# THE CIDER MAKER'S WIFE

The Cider Maker's Wife © Copyright 2018 by Evelyn Luck

Design: © Shirley Reeves

ISBN: 978-1-9996454-0-3

A catalogue record of this book is available from the British Library.

First Edition: March 2018

My Country Publications
Whites, Woodend,
Redbrook Street
Woodchurch, Kent
TN26 3QU

Email: info@mycountrypublications.com

Website: www.mycountrypublications.com

*Evelyn, Toby and Mixer.*

# THE CIDER MAKER'S WIFE

## By Evelyn Luck

My Country Publications

# Contents

Introduction ............................................................. *xiii*

In The Beginning ................................................... 1

Family .................................................................... 2

Primary School ..................................................... 5

Homewood House ................................................. 7

Children at Play ..................................................... 11

Heronden Old House ............................................. 13

Home Entertainments ........................................... 18

Limericks ............................................................. 20

My Teenage Years ................................................ 22

Animals & Family ................................................ 25

Getting Together With Bob .................................... 29

Stag Hunting - The Meet ...... ................................ 32

Dogs ..................................................................... 35

The Advent of the Crossbreed .............................. 41

Hay Making .......................................................... 46

Harvest .................................................................. 52

Charcoal Burning ................................................. 64

Root Vegetables and Peas ...................................... 71

Hops ............................................................. 73

Modern Day Hop Farming ........................................ 85

The Railway .................................................... 87

The War ........................................................ 93

The War Prisoner ............................................... 96

Water .......................................................... 97

Heronden Farm Cottages ......................................... 99

Animals ........................................................ 103

Sheep .......................................................... 108

Sheep Dipping .................................................. 110

Cattle ......................................................... 115

Driving Cattle to Camber ....................................... 119

Chickens ....................................................... 121

Children at Work ............................................... 123

Fruit .......................................................... 125

Threshing and other Winter Tasks ............................... 129

Bob and I ...................................................... 132

Cider Making ................................................... 147

Julie's Wedding ................................................ 168

Holidays ....................................................... 174

A New Beginning ................................................ 184

# Evelyn Luck's Family Tree

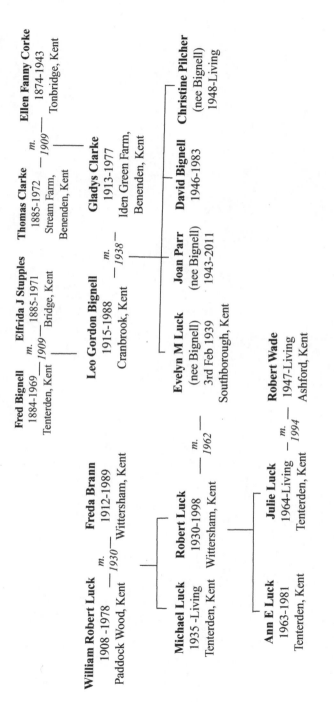

*For Julie, Robert and Christine...*

# Introduction

This book has been written in my native language, the Kentish dialect. Some readers may not be familiar with some words. I have explained their meaning in brackets. Little research has been done in preparing this work as it consists of my personal memories and experiences.

Cider making is mentioned in this book several times. A more descriptive account of the whole cider making process can be found in my earlier book entitled 'As Luck Would Have It'. This is available from My Country Publications and also Amazon.

**Evelyn Luck**

# The Cider Maker's Wife

# In The Beginning

I wasn't born in Tenterden but my roots are in Tenterden. My maternal grandfather Tom Clarke, moved from Iden Green (Farm), Benenden in 1917, together with his wife Ellen and three children – Evelyn, the eldest, after whom I was named, Tom and my mother Gladys, the youngest.

They came to Heronden Farm, Tenterden which is off the Smallhythe Road and now part of the Morghew Estate. I spent the first 23 years of my life there, on 400 acres.

My father's family also came to Tenterden at about the same time from Cranbrook and they settled in Homewood Cottages which are opposite Homewood School. My grand-father Fred Bignell managed and then bought a fish shop in Tenterden, No. 35 High Street which was 'East', the clothes shop.

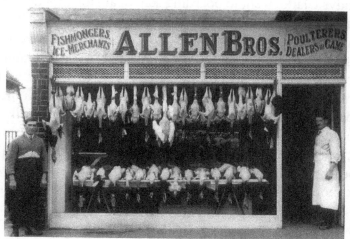

*The Fishmongers shop at 35 High Street, Tenterden which my grandfather Fred Bignell owned. He is standing in the doorway.*

1

# Family

My ancestral families had known one another for many years. The Clarkes, Lucks and Brann's being from generations of farmers. Bignells being Fishmongers and Poulterers. Grandfather Bignell served in the Veterinary Corps in WWI. Grandfather Clarke did a spell in the Territorial Army as a young man and was based at Shorncliffe Barracks. Jim and Min Brann, my future husband Bob's maternal grandparents owned the Woolpack Hotel in Tenterden in the 1930s and 1940s. Michael, Bob's younger brother was born there in 1935.

From an early age, the families were closely linked. My mother and father socialised with Bob Luck Snr and Freda Brann long before either couple married. My mother Gladys Clarke went to boarding school at Horsmonden with Vera Luck, Father-in-law's sister.

Mother and Father married in 1938 and took a wet fresh fish shop in Southborough, Tonbridge as that was my father's profession and I was born there. Of course, Mother was a farmer's daughter. At the outbreak of war in 1939 Mother's mother was very ill and Grandfather Clarke asked her if she would come home and look after her because he couldn't cope with 400 acres and a sick wife. The shop was sold in Southborough and we came home to Heronden when I was six months old, and that was my home until I got married in 1962.

Father had to change from being a fishmonger and poulterer to farming. He found it quite difficult, to begin with. One of his first experiences was to hand-milk the cows.

*Three generations - Father Leo, myself and Grandma Clarke.*

*This picture shows my grandfather's Fishmonger shop when the front was open and you could view the fish from each side of the central display.*

Armed with a three-legged stool and a galvanised bucket, he proceeded to tackle his first cow. Although the cow was quiet, a dual purpose shorthorn and easy to milk, things did not go quite to plan.

Dad was a stranger to the animal which made her nervous. Efforts to placate her, by talking softly and stroking her back made little difference. Every time dad set the stool and placed the bucket under her, she moved away, knocking over the stool and putting her foot in the bucket. After several attempts and giving the cow some food to distract her, the milking began. After a while, dad got the rhythm right and the milk flowed.

I am the oldest of four children. I was born in February 1939. My sister Joan was born in February 1943, brother David in May 1946 and Christine, youngest sister in April 1948. Sadly, David died at the age of 37 in 1983 and Joan passed away at the age of 68 in July 2011.

# Primary School

I first started school after the war and I was then six years old. Father used to ride me on the back of his bike in the carrier from Heronden up to the National Primary School which is now the Day Centre in Tenterden, Kent. I didn't like school at all. I'd been running on 400 acres on the land with my parents and to be taken away and shut up in this class-room didn't go down at all well.

So for a few days, I cried and screamed to go back home. I got away with it for a few days and then the teacher said, "Right, we're going to be firm," and she took me from my father and told him to go home and said, "she's staying here". After a while, I settled down and the teacher helped me to settle in by getting me to do demonstrations of work on the farm, like broadcasting corn. She had me marching up and down the classroom carrying a pretend basket of corn in front of me and, using both hands, throwing the corn to either side.

As well as not liking school I hated school dinners. So on most days, Mother would send something up with Father when I went to school. He would take it to the fish shop to his mum. Grandmother would come and fetch me at lunchtime and take me back to the shop and so I had my meals there. Sometimes I was treated to a piece of fish, but mostly it came from the farm.

I did eventually settle down at primary school and I did alright. Dad or Grandfather would take me to school until I was about 10 years old. Sister Joan was at school then so we used to walk together except in bad weather when we would be taken in whichever vehicle was available. Not the tractor.

When we walked, the route taken was following the lane from Heronden to the Smallhythe Road, about 1½ miles, cross the road onto Three Fields footpath and into Bells Lane, coming out onto the High Street by the then Eight Bells pub (now Café Rouge), and close to my grandparents' (Bignell's) fish shop. We would cross the High Street (not many vehicles in 1949) into Church Road, the school was at the far end opposite the church. Total distance just under two miles.

In the summertime, the route was cross-country, from Heronden to Plummer Farm, into Plummer Lane, past West View Hospital, originally the old workhouse, across the main road (now the A28) and up the High Street.

About halfway up the High Street on the western side stood an old manor house. On my way home in the summer afternoons, I always liked to pause there for a while. There was a low brick wall with red rambler roses along it. In the background positioned outside the manor house on the path was a large cage containing a green parrot who could talk a little. I was quite fascinated by this bird.

In my 11th year, exams had to be taken to gain a place in Ashford Grammar School. The exams were in two parts. I passed the first part with flying colours, but to get to Ashford Grammar School I would have to be in Tenterden by 8 am to catch the bus to Ashford. No thank you. I did not pass the second part of the exams. The same thing occurred when I was 13. The school in question then was Maidstone Technical School.

While at Primary school we were taken to church once a week for a service conducted by the vicar. On Empire Day, May 24th, the whole school was taken to the Embassy Cinema (now in 2018, M & Co clothes shop) to watch films about the Commonwealth, mainly Australia and New Zealand.

# Homewood House

Homewood House was built in 1776 by the Haffenden family who were strong Baptists. The house probably takes its name from the woodland which was part of the old estate, comprising a fine avenue of chestnut trees, sequoias and grey poplars.

The house was, until 1947, the home of Lady Amy Gertrude Drury who was the second wife of the late Admiral Sir CC Drury. Both are buried in Tenterden cemetery.

Lady Drury died at the age of 97 in 1953: the house and estate were sold to the local council to be used specifically as a school.

Admiral Sir Charles Carter Drury was a Canadian who rose from Sub-Lieutenant to Admiral and was as Captain, appointed Commanding Officer of HMS Hood in 1895. This was the third ship of that name which served in the Mediterranean until the First World War began when it was deliberately sunk outside Portland Harbour to deter German submarines and is there to this day. Sir Charles was also Second Lord of the Admiralty and Aide-de-Camp to Queen Victoria from 1897-99.

Dad had the run of Homewood House at the time belonged to Lady Drury. He was able to tell me about some of the rooms in the house. In 1948 it was turned into a school. After graduating from Primary School I started secondary school there aged 11 years in 1950. (See photo page 9).

There was a long corridor at the back of the house and we had a small room there, where we used to change for P.T. Father said, that used to be the butler's pantry. Having the run of the house and the grounds, he knew it quite well. He had three brothers and a sister and they all used to play together, especially down the back of Silverhill where the path runs from the school down to what is now the Fire Station.

Autumn Term started at the beginning of September which coincided with hop-picking beginning at about the same time. I very rarely went to school during September, and so it was when I began school at Homewood in 1950.

An entrance exam had to be taken to determine which class I was to be in. There were three levels: A, B and C. The exam proved me eligible for Class 1A. Figure 1 indicated the year. I remained in the A bracket throughout my time at Homewood.

The school was divided into four houses; Caxton, Drury, Hales and Terry. I was put in Hales.

**Caxton**    William Caxton. The first printer reputed to have been born in Tenterden.

**Drury**    Lady Drury. The former owner of Homewood House.

**Hales**    Named after Sir Edward Hales 4th Jacobite Earl of Tenterden (1758-1829).

**Terry**    Dame Ellen Terry. The actress who lived at Smallhythe Place, now preserved as a Museum.

Each house was allocated a colour as follows:
Caxton – green, Drury – blue, Hales – red, Terry – yellow.
We all wore badges accordingly.

I was never a fast runner, but I did play Cricket, Hockey and Netball. I could teach my classmates in Rural Science.

To get to Homewood School, I walked from Heronden to Tenterden Town Hall, caught the service bus to school. Fare 1d – one old penny. Coming home, I boarded the coach that took children to and from Wittersham. I then got off on the Smallhythe Road.

*Homewood School photo 1950, aged 11 years.*

I left school aged 15 when school broke up for Easter 1954, with no qualifications whatsoever. All I wanted to do was to get to work on the farm. My mother did not like this at all, wanting me to have an office job. Had this happened it would have been like caging a wild animal as I had had the freedom of 400 acres all my life. Mum's father consoled and assured her by saying, "She'll be alright". And I was, and still am.

Grandfather was my second dad. He looked after me as well as my father did. All four of us say the same. Grandfather was just there, he looked after us.

Dad was easy, if you'd got a problem, you could go and talk to him. He was a good dad, take nothing away from him, but Grandfather was the governor. He used to keep us in order too. At the meal table I was positioned next to him and if it got a bit noisy, he'd flick me in my ear, "Be quiet, will you." You did what he told you but he didn't knock you about. You might get your legs slapped if you were naughty.

Mother had a little hazel stick up on the mantelpiece. If that came down on the table, look out. Apart from that, she ruled us with her tongue.

When Joan had left school and we were going about, Mum would say, "If I find you two girls in that pub, that's the last time you go out. The blokes in there, they're only thinking about one thing!"

Joan wasn't interested in farming, she had mainly shop jobs. Her first job was at Little Fowlers Nursing Home at Hawkhurst. (Christine was born there).

Joan later worked for Woolworths and Bowketts the bakers in Tenterden. After her marriage to Reg Parr, they lived in Zambia for several years where Reg was a fitter on the Earth Movers in the copper mines. Karen was born in Zambia, Suzanne in the UK.

My brother David joined Capt Bennet at Little Bedgebury Farm, High Halden, cycling to and fro daily. He returned to work at Heronden after I married. David married Pat Standen. They farmed together at Maynes Farm, Wittersham until his death in 1983. They had three children, Jane, Denis and Tom.

When Christine left school she worked as a secretary for Cecil Burt who had a site in Judges Yard, now Judges Close in Appledore Road, where he produced rippers for bulldozers. Christine is now married to Ivan Pilcher. They live and farm at Butlers Farm, Woodchurch and in addition run a large contracting business, together with eldest son Harvey, mainly earth moving, building lakes, reservoirs, ditching and roadworks. They also have a second son Vernon and a daughter Rosemary.

# Children at play

The Homewood Estate land was the illicit playground of the many local children. The sloping footpath that separates the back of the houses in Silverhill was fenced off from the estate, and the pathway, complete with holes in the fence, represented part of every local child's domain.

Unlike today, with their skateboards and bicycles, children had to make not only their own entertainment but their equipment as well. A common toy would be an old cycle wheel, with or without the tyre, being guided onwards at the trot with a short stick. Best of all was, of course, the Go-cart, probably the precursor of the real thing.

The Go-cart was a plank of wood with an apple box nailed on the back, over a pair of old pram wheels. The front steering mechanism was another smaller plank fitted cross-wise at the front by a central bolt over a further set of pram wheels and controlled by a piece of stout rope. Only the most ingenious lads or lasses could devise brakes.

It was on one such device that my dad, Leo, playing with his brothers Jack and Harry, had his first experience of speed and excitement. Being a boy, he was only too keen to give this homemade vehicle, so-called, a try.

Silverhill path seems like a gentle slope but to a child, it was the San Moritz of Kent and sitting snug in the apple box he set off at a slow roll – to begin with anyway. Soon, he gathered speed and as there was no way – other than spoiling school shoes – of stopping, speed then was to be enjoyed.

After some minutes Leo was doing a fair whack, probably 8mph, and enjoying every minute of it, until at his maximum speed there out in front trudging along was Mr Crittenden. None of Leo's shouts were heeded and disaster followed as he ploughed into the back of the old man's legs, scooping him up, to his immense shock, and continuing as a twosome, with slightly less glamour than the two-man bobsleigh.

Had the old man not been stone deaf he may well have jumped clear.

*My brother David starting early drink/driving at the age of 2 in 1948, in a cart similar to the one my father built.*

# Heronden Old House

Heronden Farm was one of three farms owned by my grand-father Tom Clarke, the other two being Pigeon Hoo and Little Kensham at Rolvenden. Heronden Farm, known as Heronden Old House, consisted of 400 acres of good arable grassland and woodland bordering onto the lower levels of the marsh up to the Newmill Channel.

The main house had six bedrooms, a lumber-room, an attic and a cellar.

There were two reception rooms with a passageway off to the right opposite the living room, leading to an office at the end. There were cupboards along the way and on the right-hand side of the north wall there was a large walk-in pantry.

The age of the refrigerator had not arrived but the stone floor kept everything cool. There was a meat safe up above, the front of which was made of zinc with tiny holes, to let the air in, but keep the flies out. Meat, butter and cheese would be kept in there. The large shelves below the safe were wooden.

Another item was a large crock with a wooden lid for the bread, which if my mother didn't bake, would be delivered two or three times a week from the bakers in the town called Goldsmiths. (There is still a bakery on this site today.) Nina Goldsmith was Mayor of Tenterden on more than one occasion.

Everything else, fruit and veg, salted down preserves was kept on or near the floor to be cool, with pride of place being my mother's home-made lemonade.

13

The next room along, was what used to be an old dairy, again with wooden shelves and either a brick or stone floor. That was used for all manner of things – a storeroom for food and Grandfather used to cure the pork in there by salting it. He used to smoke it outside.

The material used for home smoking bacon in wartime was as follows: one 45-gallon metal oil drum (barrel) with both ends removed, using a hammer and cold chisel. Paper and kindling wood, one spile (fencing stake), some thick twine and a wet sack plus bags of oak sawdust obtained from local sawmills (British Gates). A level patch of bare earth.

First, a small fire is made, when well alight, a sawdust cover reduces fire to smoke. The cylinder-like oil drum is placed upright over the fire. The spile lays across the top of the drum. The meat is hung over the smoke, secured to the spile with the twine. The wet sack is placed over the drum top to keep the smoke in.

The smoking process would take 2 or 3 days, depending on the size of the meat.

This simple procedure normally worked well, however, things did not always go to plan.

Late one afternoon, the family were returning home and as the farmhouse came into view, clouds of smoke could be seen billowing from what appeared to be the corner of the house. Fearing the house was on fire, father driving, accelerated quickly. Utter relief was felt when it was not the house. The fire smoking the bacon had broken through its sawdust coat, the heat made the fat run, fuelling the fire somewhat.

The usual lower rooms of the house comprised a large brick floored scullery with a built-in copper. There was a duck's nest fire basket with iron bars which supported endless cooking pots. Faggots that were used for fuel were coppiced chestnut heads bound together with hazel wisps.

*Heronden House as it was in 1967.*

*Heronden as it is today.*

The reception rooms were smart and included a dining and a drawing room, and then there were the stairs up to the bedrooms. There was a skylight either side of the roof which lit the stairs and landing. There were five main bedrooms and a smaller one. I always shared a big double bed with my sister Joan in one of the larger rooms. I slept there until I got married. We had the bedroom which looked out over the garden towards Rolvenden. There was no heating. When it was cold in winter you could write your name on the ice on the inside of the window. We didn't suffer though. What you never have, you never miss. We all had feather beds which kept us warm and cosy during the night.

There was a bathroom upstairs, but no water. Cisterns had been placed there, ready for use, but they'd never been connected.

Bath night wasn't without its economies. We kids used an old tin bath in front of the fire in the living room once a week. The copper was filled with water and heated by burning faggots. Starting with the youngest we children each took our turn in the bath and got dried afterwards in front of the range with nice warm towels. There was a bath upstairs but water had to be carried upstairs for my mum and dad, and grandfather.

The house had two flush toilets, unusual for the times, however, they had to be flushed using buckets as there was no connected water.

Despite the luxury of the two toilets, Heronden Old House was big and cold, so leaving a warm bed in the middle of the night and finding a light to make the journey to one of the toilets, was not even a consideration. The norm in those days was the use of a chamber pot carefully kept under the bed. There was nothing unusual in these items of convenience sometimes being affectionately named 'Po', 'Mickey', 'Gusunder', 'Jerry' etc.

The items themselves were often plain white and robust; some pretentious or more refined families would have attractively designed ones with perhaps red roses, honey-suckle or spring flowers on them – anything that might detract from the real use of the item.

My then future father-in-law, Bob Luck senior, had a rare musical one - not that the china ones didn't ring when they were being used - but one that had a wind-up musical box that played a tune called 'Blue-eyed Sally'.

## Blue-eyed Sally - By Colin Roberts

*The chamber pot he bought was best*
*Indeed, a cut above the rest,*
*Attached to a music box, much improved*
*That played aloud when it was moved.*
*'Blue-eyed Sally' the tune's refrain,*
*When played at night, no one complained,*
*And so such musical contemplation*
*Accompanied nocturnal micturition.*

Old Bob answered the door with this chamber pot in his hand one day only to find it was the curate from St Mildred's.

Toilet tissues during the war did not exist and the best homemade facilities were often the daily newspapers cut into squares by all the kids and hung conveniently on a nail. The nearest that one came to luxury was the soft blue paper sometimes wrapped around oranges when they were available.

There was a large cellar, the entrance of which was in the middle of the house with steps going down. It wasn't used very much for storage because it was a bit on the damp side.

In wartime, we slept down in the cellar on deck chairs, camp beds and makeshift beds.

# Home Entertainments

As there was no electricity at Heronden, our only links with the outside media world were via telephone, newspapers and the radio (wireless) – battery operated. A spare was always kept because when flat the battery had to be taken to Tenterden to be recharged - Potters I think.

In summer we four were always amusing ourselves outside, making camps, searching for birds nests, just to see how many species we could find. The Lapwing, whose nest was just a hollow on the ground. If the nest contained four eggs with the points together, we knew the bird was incubating. A hollow tree is where the owl made a home, while the songbirds occupied the hedges.

In the winter evenings it was 'I Spy', 'Hide and Seek', 'Ludo', 'Snakes & Ladders'; jigsaws, colouring and drawing

*Home Entertainment - Joan, myself and two local children building camps.*

books; card games from 'Happy Families' and 'Snap' to more sophisticated games as we became older. We also played darts.

The first time I visited the cinema – The Embassy in Tenterden – I was a teenager and went with a friend. The film showing was the western, *'Red River'*.

In addition to that already listed, we interacted letters and figures to form riddles and rhymes, such as:

"How do you spell 'hungry horse' in 4 letters? mtgg.

ICUR, ICUB, ICUR, 2Ys4 ME

*David, Christine, myself and Joan with Father Christmas 1955.*

## Limericks

There was an old man of Kent,
Whose legs where remarkably bent,
So, to save any trouble,
He always walked double,
So, when he was coming, he went.

There was an old lady of Ewhurst,
Who was riding a bike and it threw her,
A butcher came by and said "Missus don't cry"
And fastened her on with a skewer.

*Tenterden Young Farmers Club about 1961, in the Town Hall with the sign someone had taken from the Woolpack Hotel.*

*Winner of the Calf Rearing competition in the late 1950s. Picture taken at Goldwell Farm, Biddenden.*

# My Teenage Years

On leaving school in 1954 I started to work full-time on the farm. I joined Tenterden Young Farmers Club straightaway, it was a big, active club. The meeting place used to be the old St John's Ambulance hut on Golden Square. My friend Mavis Morris, who was living at Plummer Farm then which adjoined Heronden, was already a member and she got me into it.

Grandfather's relaxation was to go to Tenterden Club to play a game of snooker, he would give me a lift to Tenterden where I would meet Mavis.

Then, when the meeting was over I would walk back to the club for a ride home. In summertime, I'd walk home with Mavis across the fields.

The meetings were weekly. In the winter we'd meet indoors (I remember we went to Chilham Paper Mills one time), and in the summer the meetings would be on different farms, to experience the different aspects of farming.

I was Assistant Secretary for a couple of years and then Secretary. Altogether I was part of the Young Farmers Club for five years or so, up until about 1961.

Sometimes we used to go to the pub after meetings and we also held quizzes. There was a Young Farmers Club Ball in the Town Hall.

I also joined the Old Time Dance Club, held in the big room upstairs at the Vine in Tenterden. Charlie Tonbridge and his wife (who used to run the Cornex Garage in Rolvenden) organised it. We learned dances like the Gay Gordons and the Valeta. I've never been much of a dancer but it was an evening out and a bit of fun. All age groups enjoyed the evening's dances.

Bob wasn't a member of Young Farmers or the Old Time Dance Group, but he went to the Kent Farm Institute at Sittingbourne, which is now known as Hadlow College.

On Mondays, I always had to help Mother do the washing. Everything was done by hand, although we had a mangle. The last rinse had a cube of Reckitt's Blue crumbled into the water to bring out the white. After having been put through the old cast iron mangle with large wooden rollers, it looked more like a cider press. The laundry was then hung out on the line to dry.

My grandfather held Game Shoots at Heronden to which the two Bob Lucks (father and son, known as Old Bob and Young Bob) were invited. It was an incident at one of these shoots that my first real memory of Young Bob was captured. I was 11 or 12 years old. Bob was 8½ years my senior.

The pheasants were being driven to the top of Gazedown Wood which had a large pond on its eastern fringe. One of the guns dropped a bird which fell into the water. A spaniel was sent to retrieve it. The dog located the dead bird picked it up and turned back towards the bank, taking a slightly different route, straight into some willow growing some way out. The dog became wedged in between two trunks. Getting lower in the water it was feared the dog would drown. Like me, Young Bob loved all animals and this dog was not going to die. He stripped off his top clothes and dived into the very cold water. (Pheasant shooting has a season from 1st October to 1st February.) Swimming strongly, he soon reached the stricken dog, lifting it up to where the trunks were wider apart. Released and relieved, the dog still holding the pheasant, swam back to its owner, while everyone applauded both dog and rescuer.

Another of the guns took off his overcoat and gave Bob a good rub down. All then moved off for the final drive that day. Then we went back to the farmhouse for refreshments which my mother and I had prepared earlier.

# Animals and Family

My mother grew up with the cart horses and rode to hounds (hunting). She was a good horsewoman. Mum taught me to ride and drive a pony when I was about 10 years old. My first pony was Molly, a black Shetland-cross which had a long woolly coat in winter. She was a ride and drive pony. As well as riding, she pulled a tub cart. We used this to get us four kids to the far reaches of the farm. Christine was a toddler, and the pony and cart were much easier transport than a pushchair. At haymaking and harvest times this transport was used to take refreshments to the farm workers because work would continue until dusk. Work was at that time still very manual and labour-intensive.

Having outgrown Molly, I moved on to a grey Irish cob mare which we named Silver Shadow. She had to work for her living and after leaving school I used her to do the 'lookering', checking all the livestock were right in number and health. Often I would do this late in the day, especially in hot weather, when all the animals were grazing in the evening. From horseback, they are easier to count and detect lameness or a 'mislaid' sheep. This is when a sheep lies down on uneven ground and is unable to right itself.

Then I started competing in shows and gymkhanas. I won my first cup with Shadow for the Best Turned-Out Pony looked after by its owner/rider. We also followed the Ashford Valley foxhounds.

In my late teens, Mother heard of a thoroughbred mare that was for sale near Hythe. We went to try her and she came home with us. She was quite well bred for flat racing being sired by *Robert Barker* out of the mare *Stolen Love* who was of Irish descent. She was bred by Mr Jabez Barker, owner of the stallion. The sire and the dam's names were put together. Her registered name was *Roberts Love*. Her stable name was Stardust. She was never successful at flat racing due to a skin complaint that made training difficult.

When I married, father-in-law wouldn't have a horse on the place, so I had to sell her and she went to Dick Offen who was in Biddenden at that time. He was a dealer and he sold her to a lady near Dover and she went showing.

Then I lost track of her. We knew that she was trained by a Tom Griffiths because we had all her records. One day Bob was out delivering cider. On returning home he said, "You know Tom Griffiths who trained your horse, he's just taken the Carpenter's Arms pub at Mayfield". Bob and I drove to visit him and have a chat about the horse. Sometime later, one of the women Tom Griffiths used to train for bought her and she had gone back to Winchester Stud where she had been born. Her second foal, named *Billy Strong* was by *Pinza*, on whom Sir Gordon Richards had won the 1953 Derby, and she was in foal to him again, who was named *Pintov*. *Billy Strong* and *Pintov* both had successful careers NH Racing over hurdles. The mare had had a 2-year-old colt by *Indigenous* named *Native Copper*. He had already been placed twice in flat races, but unfortunately broke a front leg when going for a win. The owner of the mare, *Robert's Love*, a Mrs Hunt, needed to register the mare in the General Stud Book to give pedigree recognition to her offspring. All owners had to be traced to achieve this. Dick Offen was at first uncooperative, but I went to see him and he did indeed help to obtain a successful registration.

Bob and I, Ann and Julie went to visit Mrs Hunt and my ex-mare and her foals at Sparsholt near Winchester. She was

*Me on Stardust (Robert's Love) in approximately 1957.*

*Reunited with my old mare.*

*Native Copper her first foal*

*Her second foal Billy Strong.*

*Robert's Love with owner Mr Hunt.*

by *Robert Barker* out of *Stolen Love* = *Robert's Love*. No wonder I called her Stardust.

While visiting Tom Griffiths at the Carpenter's Arms, Bob and I got to know the jockeys associated with the trainer, namely R.P. (Bobby) Elliot, Geoff Lewis and Geordie Ramshaw. All were successful in their day. Geoff Lewis went on to train many winners.

# Getting Together With Bob

During the winter time, the marsh would flood and wild duck (Mallards) were regular visitors. Grandfather used to enjoy a bit of shooting and he also liked the ducks to eat. It was called 'flight shooting' and took place either in the morning or the early evening: when the birds flew in for the night to feed, and then in the morning when they flew off.

In 1959 Grandfather sold 200 acres to Bob's father. We started going out when I was about 18. I'm not quite sure exactly how and when it happened. Bob would come down to Heronden in the evenings with some corn to feed the ducks and I used to go with him as I knew the lay of the land.

The ducks came in when there was a little bit of water on top of the grass. It's called 'slop water'. We would put the feed where we knew the ducks would fly in.

My mother said to Bob, "I don't know what you have that I haven't because I have more difficulty in getting Evelyn to feed the chicken than you have feeding ducks.

In 1958/59 we were going about together. Then around hop-picking time, in the autumn of 1959, I suddenly got stood up one night. We were going to Hastings and Dad dropped me off on his way to collect the hops from Rolvenden, so that Bob could pick me up. But when Dad came back I was still waiting, so instead I went to Pigeon Hoo with Dad to unload the hops. Bob came up with some excuse, but that was the end of it for the time being. His dad didn't like that I'd been stood up one bit.

But, that was that. I found another boyfriend for about a year, though it wasn't the same.

Bob's birthday was on 17th August and one evening in August I was out with this other chap at the Ewe & Lamb in Rolvenden for a drink. My mother used to call this chap 'elastic mind' because he wouldn't stretch any further than Rolvenden. Anyway, we were in the pub and in came Bob with one of his mates. We got talking and had a drink together.

I asked Bob if he was coming down to the farm the next day.

"Why?" he asked.

"Well, I've got something for you and I can't post it."

"What's it for?"

"Well, it's for your birthday."

It went quiet for a minute, and he said, "Well, you'd better come to Hastings tomorrow night."

I thought, this isn't too bad, I'm here with one bloke and making a date with another!

So, the next night, Wednesday, he came to Herondon in the Land Rover to pick me up en route to Hastings delivering the cider (Bob wasn't stupid, he had me doing the paperwork writing out the invoices), and so I gave him his present, but I didn't know if he was going to like it or not.

The next night Dad went up to The Cellars in Tenterden. He came home and said to me, "I've just seen Young Bob in the town, and he said, he can lay in bed and shoot ducks now". So I reckoned that he liked his present. And the rest is history.

[*Picture: Poachard Rising, See page 31.*]

The Cider Maker's Wife

*'Poachards Rising' a watercolour by Vernon Wood, bought in Horace Ashdown's shop, next door to what was the police office in Tenterden.*

## Stag Hunting - The Meet

A hunt meet was, and still is, a spectacular event.

The Master, Master of the Stag Hounds (MSH) the Huntsman, who sounds the horn and the Whipper-In, controller of the hounds, all wearing their red coats (Hunting Pink) arrive with the hounds at the pub, the Black Horse, now the William Caxton in Tenterden. The Master, riding a strong grey gelding, the Huntsman on a big bay while the Whipper-In is astride a lively chestnut, soon the field begin to assemble, those who follow the hounds on horseback (Riding to Hounds). A waiter emerges from the pub with a tray of drinks (the stirrup cup) to offer to the riders.

The riders range from children on lead-rein ponies, who will probably follow until the stag is located, to teenagers on smartly turned out mounts with manes and tails plaited.

Local farmers on quite heavy animals, reminiscent of draught horse types. The city workers riding the more modern hunter, and of course the Lady riding side-saddle, elegant in a black riding habit on a noble-spirited gelding.

Soon it is time to move off in search of the stag. The huntsman blows the horn, then hounds give tongue (bark) and horses neigh with excitement and set off at a brisk trot, to locate the released stag.

The Mid Kent Staghounds were active in this area up to the mid-1950s. The staghounds were then disbanded and merged with the Ashford Valley Foxhounds. Deer were bred specially for hunting, once they had reached maturity.

One stag would be taken out in the stag cart and released into the open countryside about an hour or so before the hounds met at the nearby pub.

After the meet, led by the huntsman, the hunt would arrive at the location of the released stag. Picking up the scent hounds were soon in full cry. Although the stag is in unfamiliar countryside, its speed and jumping ability is far superior to that of horse and hound, taking hedges, gates, fences, ditches, even the Newmill Channel in its stride.

The hounds baulked at the Newmill Channel, losing the scent and not wanting to cross the deep, fast-flowing water. The channel was the stags salvation.

The Hounds return home while the stag is left to wander the countryside and becomes an outlier.

Of course, the hunt does not like to be defeated and will come for it again, but this was nearly the end of the hunting season which meant it would be the following Autumn at least before the hunt could try again.

Meanwhile, the stag had come back to Heronden and in a grassy sloping field surrounded on three sides by woodland,

*Ashford Valley Hunt with Ann on Julie's horse, 'High Jinks'.*

a stream running through the wood at the bottom a large pond at the top, shelter also in the form of a few hawthorn bushes, there the stag made its home.

Come late Autumn, the master and huntsman came to the farm seeking the stag. They found the lair, saw where it had laid, identified the hoof prints (known as slots).

This animal had now been living out in the area for about 8 months and knew it well, grazing with the sheep and cattle, hopping over the channel at will, but always returned to the field it made home.

The hunt came, the stag's sharp ears caught the clip-clop of hooves as hounds and followers trotted along Smallhythe Road, only a short distance across the fields. A whiff of scent from horse and hound. Danger! The stag was away, bounding through the wood, galloping across the meadows, scaling hedges and fences, down onto the marsh, 100 acres lying alongside the channel bank, running the track and jumping the water and away towards Rolvenden Layne. Safe and sound. Hounds and riders never caught a glimpse of this beautiful, elegant, agile creature.

The hunt came several times but the stag was never caught and was eventually left in peace, for a long time.

However, a farmer on the Rolvenden side of the channel, which is the boundary between Tenterden and Rolvenden, kept Friesian heifers down on the marsh. One heifer became stuck in one of the ditches and subsequently aborted her calf. The stag was blamed for chasing the heifer into the ditch, but there was no proof. The animal had a quiet, almost lazy manner and no such behaviour had ever been seen in the time it had been running free.

The farmer was not willing to do anything other than having this regal creature shot. Having outlived and outwitted all pursuers, there was no chance against a rifle!

# Dogs

It seems that I had an affinity with and an ability to train animals from an early age.

The first dog that I can remember was a medium-sized, smooth-coated, black mongrel bitch named Tinker. She had a lovely nature and she was my friend and playmate when Mum was busy. Heronden was quite remote. There were not any other small children around and no such thing as a nursery, pre-school group or crèche in the early 1940s.

Having regularly watched the cart horses being harnessed and put into the wagons or dung cart this intrigued me. So, I set about making a hop-string harness for the dog Tinker. A cardboard box became a cart and she willingly pulled this contraption around the house. But to my mind, this was not complete. A passenger was needed. Now at the same time, we had a ginger tom cat. No clues to the cat's name; Grandfather was Tom so it had to be Ginger. I was always carrying this poor cat around and making it beds. It was very well handled. Ginger became the passenger. There were plenty of passages within the house where I could lead Tinker and give Ginger a ride. The cat got so used to this procedure that as soon as he saw me he would jump straight into his 'cart'.

Chief was a blue roan cocker spaniel. He loved running around the farm and woods with us. One day the family went on a woodland walk into Plummer Wood which had quite a deep ditch running through it. Chief was off hunting rabbits, barking in delight. Usually, he would return to us but on this occasion, he didn't. Calling and whistling did not bring him

35

back either. It was assumed that he was trying to dig out a rabbit and not listening to us and that he would come home when he was ready. He was still missing next morning. Dad went to look for him, retracing the route taken the previous day. He was found dead in the ditch. Chief had obviously jumped the ditch in full flight, collided with a tree which stunned him, fallen into the ditch and drowned. Dog owners beware.

There have of course been many dogs in my life and that of my late husband. Bob got his first Jack Russell Terrier in the early 1950s. She was named Vicky and was bred by Bill Deedes who was Conservative MP for Ashford for many years and was also Editor of the Daily Telegraph. She was what is known as a working terrier – went to earth to flush out foxes. She was a clever little dog, brave too. Unfortunately, she met her death when she entered a rabbit burrow which had been excavated by foxes. She was suffocated by four cubs. Her daughter, Penny, was also in the burrow but she was dug out just in time. The two had been underground for nearly 24 hours. To lose a well-loved animal, whether it be by accident, illness or old age, is always a heart-rending experience and one never gets used to it.

There comes a time when all of us must make a decision about having a pet put down. It is hard to do, but usually, you will know when that time comes, at least it is the last kind thing that you, the owner, can do. Some people feel that to get another dog soon after losing one is disloyal and unfeeling. No, that animal can't be replaced, it never can be, but my advice is, get another, move on because a dog's life is so much shorter compared to human life. Any dog you may have owned will be in your heart and mind forever. That is why I am able to tell of these special loving companions it has been my great privilege to have known over the years.

Being on the farm we had Collies as well as terriers. The last one, Bessie, passed away in 1986, aged 16 years.

In 1977, terrier Vicky III was diagnosed with sugar diabetes. The vet warned us that she would soon go blind and she was losing weight too. We were advised to look for another pup. Bob located a litter out at Wadhurst. At the beginning of June, she was ready to leave for her new home. Bob collected her, a black and white rough-coated ball of fluff. She was duly named Whisky (Black & White Whisky). There was just one problem. Ann, our elder daughter, didn't like her after Vicky, her smooth-coated predecessor. It so happened that the farrier I was using at that time had a litter. We all met at the August Ashford Valley Terrier Show to choose the pup, Ann's choice. The pup being tan and white became Shandy.

Everything was fine, for a few months. One day Julie, then aged 13, came home from school in tears. It took me days to get out of her what was upsetting her. At last, it all spilt out: "Mum, you and Dad have got a puppy, and so has Ann, I haven't got one." Oh dear.

Our dwelling at Mill Pond Farm was a two-bedroom Colt bungalow. Completely made of cedar wood manufactured by W.H. Colt at Bethersden, hence Colt bungalow. Built in 1956.

Bob said that we could not have a fourth dog in this small place, but Julie would not let it go, showing me adverts in the local paper and how she intended to care for a puppy and that it would not take up much space. It was now the end of November, not the best of times to take in a puppy.

I knew our mate Bill Waters had a litter of Jack Russells. Taking Julie, I went to see him. There were two left. Julie took a fancy to the little bitch. I explained to her that the puppy was not old enough to leave its mother. She would have to wait until after Christmas. I knew that it would be ready for Christmas. Now, I had to tell Bob. A few days later we were leaving the farm in the van when Bob asked me if I had seen Bill's pups and were they OK. I assured him they were good. Then added that he would be seeing one.

"What do you mean?" he asked.

I told him that Julie was to have one. He went deadly quiet, the only sound being the van engine and my heart beating as I drove. We had travelled nearly half a mile before Bob spoke. "Well, I don't really mind, do I?"

Bob met Bill on Christmas Eve, brought the puppy home and put it straight into Julie's bed with her. The puppy had little colour other than white. I said that she had dodged the paintbrush, and we had some puddles to dodge in the kitchen, so she became Dodger.

*Mixer with her puppies.*

*Mixer's puppies with Otto at the back.*

39

*Mixer's puppies being nursed by grandmother, Soda.*

*Dot, Minty, Mixer and Otto.*

# The Advent of the Crossbreed

In 1991, Mixer, who was Whisky's granddaughter, was three years old and came into season in early December. I spent Christmas taking her to a stud dog but she was not interested until Boxing Day morning when it was thought two successful matings had occurred. That evening we had a visitor. On opening the door, Mixer slipped out, unnoticed. Several minutes elapsed before we discovered her missing. She was found mated with the neighbour's Collie.

Next morning I contacted the vet for an injection to stop pregnancy but I was assured that she would have conceived to the earlier mating with the Jack Russell. How wrong could he be?

Mixer gave birth to eight Collie pups on 23rd February 1992. One did not survive. They were all black and white, like miniature Collies. Soda, Mixer's mother, had been in season at the same time and had a false pregnancy, whereby she produced milk, so the two bitches between them reared the pups until they were able to lap. When the pups were three to four weeks it was decided to keep one of the bitches. I chose one of the smaller ones which I called Dot. At eight weeks all went to new homes except one male pup, the firstborn, Otto.

Some Londoners came to the farm to look at a horse and they wanted to take him home to Deptford. I would not let him go. So both Dot and Otto were kept. Bob had great delight in telling all his mates how he now had a new breed of dog, namely a pair of Trollies (Terrier and Collie). This I think inadvertently was the start of the designer dog breeds, eg. Labradoodles, Cockapoos, etc.

41

I joined Sally Jay's obedience classes at Biddenden. I knew that they needed to be trained properly with expert tuition.

When Dot and Otto were six months old I entered my first Obedience show, mainly for experience for the dogs and myself. I was also a beginner in the Obedience world. (Bob and I had shown the Terriers successfully in the late 1950s to 1962.) No prizes were gained at this first attempt at Obedience but we did get a couple of rosettes in the Show section. Otto won a puppy class at a subsequent show and Dot soon after. We went on to improve and were soon in the ribbons in both Showing and Obedience.

I later joined a Ring Craft class, learning how to handle the dogs correctly in the ring. The ring craft I think led me to my proudest moment with the pair. They were two years old when I entered them in a Matched Brace Class. I was the only competitor with crossbreeds in a large class. There was every pedigree breed from Shelties to Alsatians (German Shepherd dogs).

The judge looks for conformation, condition, movement and the way they go together. Both dogs must be on your left side with both leads in your left hand. I was next to last to go, with the Shelties last. We all had to walk a triangle. Some of the first to go didn't do well and two pairs had a punch-up – Dogs, that is, not the handlers.

I was immediately called in First. I just could not believe it. My two humble little dogs beating all this pedigree lot.

The funniest moment was during a much later show. Dot and Otto were in the Advanced Obedience. We had to do a five-minute Out-of-sight Stay (the dogs are put in the sit position where they must remain while the handler disappears for the allotted time). The steward called the handlers back when time was up, to release the dogs. The Judge turned to me and said, "Your dog, Otto, got up, had a scratch and sat down again. I am sorry but I have to dock his points." No rosette for that class.

Dot had a litter of pups when she was five in 1997. Two of them had chocolate colouring in their coats. I named them Minty and Smartie. I kept Minty. She was absolutely brilliant at Showing, Obedience, and at home for foxes and rabbits. It must be remembered that these dogs of mine were all farm dogs, not bred just for showing.

In the autumn of 2005, I had the chance to rehome a Parson Terrier named Libby. She was a lovely little bitch that had had a bad start in life and at the age of 16 months, I was her fifth owner. I had had her for about a week when Dot was suddenly ill. I could see that she was in a bad way. The vet came out, he did not know what was wrong. He took her to do some tests, which proved she was fighting something massive, and she was put on a drip and antibiotics. Early the next morning the vet phoned to say Dot had died during the night. A post-mortem revealed that the cause was liver cancer. I was not there at her time of death. I found that very hard to deal with. I beat myself up over it for a long time and writing this brings tears to my eyes even now, after 12 years.

Libby was the first pedigree dog in my life. She was Kennel Club (KC) registered and came with a five generation pedigree. Libby was in poor condition but within a month she had improved so much that she was winning Terrier classes and Best in Show. She settled in well with Otto and Minty. I had great plans for her; another year Showing, then a litter of pups. So much for well-laid plans of mice and men, and women!

Early the following year Minty and Libby got into a fight over another dog. Bitches are notorious fighters and two more serious fights ensued, costing more than £300 in vet's bills. I could no longer let them be together because it meant they would kill each other. I had to find Libby another home. I knew that Bob Larthe, a local bus driver, who I had known for a long time, was looking for a dog for rabbit shooting. Bob liked her and so she went to live with him and Sylvia. Libby used to return with Bob at weekends. We all walked out together. Libby had a lovely home there until her death in December 2016.

Shortly after the sad parting from Libby in March 2006, I found a litter of stunning Parson-type terrier puppies. They were not KC registered, but it didn't matter. They were four weeks old. I decided to buy two dog pups. On my way home giving thought to names, Sam and Silas sounded ideal. As they developed it was obvious they were not true Jack Russells. At about four months they clearly showed signs of Beagle. From six months old they were winning in the show ring; Crossbreed Handsome Dog, Pairs, Best Condition and, Sam especially, Movement. They have beaten a lot of top-class dogs. At home on the farm, they hunt like Beagles and can deal with anything from a mouse to a fox. This hunting instinct has led to a few injuries. Sam banged his head on a concrete wall and suffered a nerve palsy. He lost the use of his jaw and was unable to eat or drink for a month. I had to put food into his mouth and administer water via a syringe. He lost all his head and facial muscles. He was very ill for about two months. Several times I thought he would die. I also wondered if it was right trying to keep him alive. He was treated with steroids. Gradually he began to improve. Massaging his head brought the muscles back. The steroids were weaned off. About a month later, aged seven, he won a veteran's class.

Silas has had his problems too, suffering glaucoma in the same year, 2014. He had his left eye removed and his right in March 2016. He manages very well around the house, garden, farmyard and fields. His nose and ears compensate for his eye loss. He still scents well and loves to get his head down a rabbit hole.

In 2010 I devastatingly lost both Otto, three weeks short of his 18th birthday and Minty, 13, within five months. Otto retired from Showing when he won a Veteran class at 17½ years of age. Minty won her last rosette about six weeks before she was diagnosed with lung cancer. Going from four dogs to two, quickly left a hole in my life and I wanted another. The matter had to be discussed with my daughter Julie because of the fact that the dogs might outlive me and then they would be her responsibility. Julie gave me the go-ahead and I promised that he would be called Dodger.

At the beginning of January 2012, my friend Patsy Bird and I went to see a litter of KC-registered Parson Terriers at Biddenden. Together we chose the best looking, outgoing pup. His registered name was King of Kings. He was 12 weeks old. Soon he was walking out with me, Sam and Silas. One day he entered a patch of undergrowth. After going to his rescue, I discovered he was actually hunting rabbits. He was headstrong right from the start. Despite an extended course of training I have never been able to make a decent dog of him. He has always been aggressive, insanely jealous and volatile. I question his parentage regularly. Despite this, he has done well in the Show ring. My hopes of competing in Open Shows were dashed when he was castrated. That did not quieten him down either. He started to run off on his own after rabbits. On one occasion, he disappeared about 3.45pm and returned at around the same time next morning. From then on, he was either confined to barracks or on the lead. Now in his seventh year, he has mellowed a little, but he still has to be caged when left or he will start a fight.

I must have made some impression because when I get really angry with him, like the ginger cat, he jumps into his box!

# Hay Making

The meadows/fields/land, whichever description is preferred, were "laid in", that is to say, that animals were excluded and therefore the areas were not grazed from the end of April/beginning of May. A period of six to eight weeks is needed for the crop to grow to maturity.

June and July are the best hay-making months. June-made hay is always the best feed quality, the grass being young, sweet and tender. Good, strong, hot sunshine plus some breeze is needed to 'cook' the grass. Once the grass is cut, it is left untouched for a few days until the colour has changed from bright green to grey-green and the upper side is dry. A shower of rain at this stage is not detrimental because the water runs off and does not penetrate the crop.

The hay is now ready for turning. In the 1920s this was still done by hand using wooden rakes, made from ash. Men, women and some children would gather to turn the hay, so that the green underside, which had yet to be exposed to the sun and air would dry. This would take another two to three days, depending on the weather and the thickness of the crop. I remember, in my early days, using a wooden hay rake and helping out as best I could. (See picture on page 47.)

In times of inclement weather, the hay was 'cocked up'. Using pitchforks and rakes, the hay was heaped up in large lumps with the sides combed down with a rake so that any rain ran off. Too much wet ruined the hay.

When the weather came right again, when the dark clouds had rolled away, and the sun rose gloriously in the eastern sky signalling a lovely glowing day, the hay was spread out

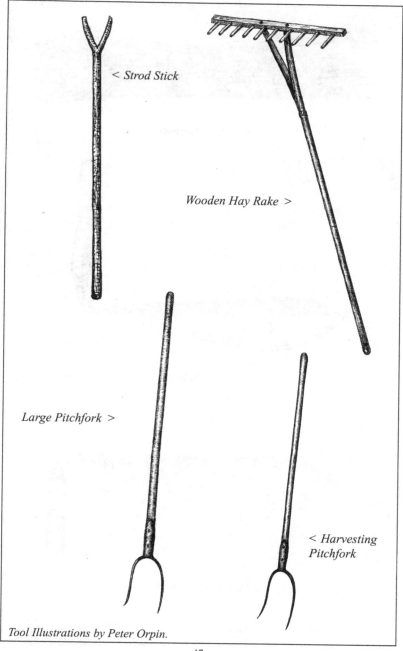

*< Strod Stick*

*Wooden Hay Rake >*

*Large Pitchfork >*

*< Harvesting Pitchfork*

*Tool Illustrations by Peter Orpin.*

*Bundle of Faggots*

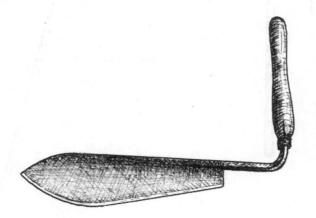

*Hay Knife*

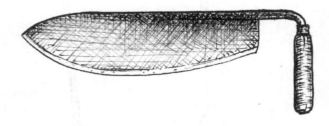

*Hay or Silage Knife*

*Tool Illustrations by Peter Orpin.*

*Stook*

*Sheaf of Corn*

on the ground. Once the hay was thoroughly dry the horses and wagon were brought out.

Basically, the wagons were built from wood, usually oak and ash, with forged iron axles. They had flat beds with removable lades and were four-wheeled with a turntable built into the front to give a 180-degree turn. Wagons could be built to accommodate one, two or three horses. Two horse wagons would have shafts wide enough for two horses side by side or a central pole where one horse stood either side. For three horses the lead horse wore chains attached to the wagon and stood centrally, ahead of the horses in the shafts.

The wheels were all wood except for the rim (tyre) which was iron. Tyres were fitted hot to the wood so that when cold and shrunken, they were held tightly in place on the wheel. The person who made wheels was known as a wheelwright.

The last one that I knew of was Pop Orpin who had a yard at the top of Rolvenden Hill on the right, adjacent to Half Crown Cottage. Wheels of all dimensions, materials and colours could be observed, mostly needing attention of some kind, from broken spokes to rims that had come adrift.

Wagons came painted in primary colours, dark red, bright blue, grass green and sunflower yellow. Some, like modern day vehicles, were adorned with the names of individual farmers or of bigger estates.

The poetic description of this type of wagon is a Hay Wain (Constable painted such a picture, which now hangs in the National Gallery).

Two magnificent Shire horses, standing 17 hands, bay, with flowing black manes and tails with white feathers about their fetlocks. Harnessed side by side, a row of horse brasses on their chests, glinting in the sunlight and the chains jingling as they walked. With a 'Whoa!' from the Wagoner (the person in charge of the draught horses) the two horses halted and stood, unheld, patiently waiting while the loose hay was loaded, using pitchforks, to the top of the wagon lades (supports to the front and rear to prevent the load falling off). Then, it was off to the farmyard to be put into the Kent Barn, usually, brick built under a tiled roof with internal woodwork making sections called bays.

Hay was also built into stacks (ricks). A stack 'foot' was made first using faggots, timber and/or straw, to prevent hay touching the ground and soaking up moisture. Round, square or oblong stacks were built depending on taste, room or co-ordination, etc. Once the season's crop was in, each stack was 'roofed', thatched using either grey reed from marsh ditches or bright gold wheat straw, reserved from the previous year's harvest, and held in place by taupe-coloured hazel battens and spars.

Farming has moved on over the last eight decades becoming more mechanised every year.

The working horse breeds; the great British Shire, mainly Bay in colour, brown body, black mane, tail and legs with white feathers and white on the face, usually a blaze; the stout, dapple grey Percheron, originally introduced to this country from the La Perche district in France; the strong Suffolk Punch, always chestnut in colour and it could outwalk any man; and from the north the lighter-built Clydesdale, similarly coloured to the Shire. All have long since disappeared from farms and are now mainly seen at shows and some ploughing matches.

From horse-drawn mowers, rakes and reapers, some of which still lie forgotten in some rural properties, we now have modern-day machinery which has evolved over the years – from the first hay baler which used wire to bind the bales to today's balers spinning out great round bales wrapped in white mesh net – and from the small conventional rectangular bales to the four and six-stringed quadrants, which only a machine can handle.

Driving around the countryside the round bales can be seen standing in barns, one on top of the other, looking like enormous columns and appearing to be supporting the roofs. Some lie in farmyards making horizontal columns. Either side can be seen similar-sized bales wrapped in black plastic, this is silage. The green grass is left to wilt for 24-48 hours before baling. It has high feed value and a very pungent smell. Then there is the pale green wrapped 'haylage'. The grass is dried more than silage but not completely. Sealing the product in plastic, which is airtight, preserves the contents.

# Harvest

July is the month which sees the beginning of harvesting when the sun is still high in the sky and has used its power to ripen the corn and bake the ground hard to allow easy access and movement over the land. The swallows dive and twirl after some elusive insect. The meadows which were lush and green just a short while ago now have a brownish tinge.

Wheat, barley and oats are ripe, and ready for harvesting when the ears are 'sickled over' and the grain is as hard as grit. Winter barley usually is the first to ripen: the seed having been sown in the autumn when the ground is still warm from the summer sun and the rooks and seagulls scan the freshly moved soil in search of tasty morsels and any seed left uncovered. The seed quickly germinates with the help of a nice shower. Oats and wheat are also winter sown but are slower to mature.

Spring wheat is the last crop to harvest. The land, ploughed in the autumn, is left fallow over the winter. This is done for a number of reasons, including allowing the winter weather to break down heavy soil such as clay, yellow or blue in colour. The latter is known as Blue Carp. It also helped to rid the field of weeds before sprays became available.

A wet October and November meant that it was then too late to sow the winter variety.

Wheat, oats and barley all have spring varieties. The ideal planting month is March when the days are lengthening and the sun has a little more power. March is the month of many kinds of weather when one can get sunburnt one day and

*Cutting corn with binder.*                    *© Richard Filmer*

*Shocks or stooks of wheat in the field. Photo courtesy of Neil Ridley.*

*Loading sheaves.*                    *Photo courtesy of Neil Ridley*

*Brian Croucher stacking bundles of thatching straw. Neil Ridley in background. Photo © Richard Filmer*

*Thatched House, Smarden in Kent. June 1996. Thatching by P. Brocklebank.*

*Threshing machine belt driven by a Standard Fordson tractor.*

*Threshing machine. Steam driven.   © Neil Ridley.*

*At harvesting time with the binder and Trixies about 1955.*

Photo © Richard Filmer

*Threshing machine. Note the shafts for horses.*

need an overcoat the next to deal with an icy blast or a sudden downpour.

Should it become April before the seed can be sown, this is known as Cuckoo Corn because it coincides with the arrival of the bird in England. Seed planted this late usually has a lower yield than that planted earlier.

The saying goes, 'March winds and April showers bring forth May flowers,' and with a little bit of luck, the crop may be better than expected.

When ripe, the barley with its whiskery ears, a little deeper in colour than the oats, but not as bright as the more golden red wheat, all shimmer in the sun with the wind moving and swaying the standing corn as though in some exotic dance.

To allow the self-binder/reaper access, first, a 'path' must be cut by hand using a scythe all around the outside of the field. This operation is called 'opening' and prevents any corn being ruined by the reaper.

A knife at the front of the binder cuts the corn, a set of rotating arms ('sweeps') pushes the corn onto a moving canvas table and it is then transported through the machine via more moving canvasses where it reaches the packers (made into 'sheaves'), bound and tied with string (the 'knotter'). The sheaf is then discharged onto the ground.

This work was done by horses pre-1940. I only remember the tractor at work and I used to sit on the binder and operate the sweeps. They had to be adjusted according to the height of the corn and I would alert the tractor driver if anything went wrong. The most common problems were if a piece of string or some object like a hard lump of earth got jammed in the knotter, then the sheaves would be thrown out loose. Of course, the same would occur if the ball of string ran out. The moving canvasses were fitted tight with leather straps over rollers. Now and then, some straw or some rubbish like the foul-smelling Mayweed would wrap around the end of the rollers which hindered the movement. This meant stopping, undoing the canvas and with a pocket knife cutting off the offending objects.

After the binder had made several circuits of the field the farm workers came out to start 'shocking up' (making 'stooks'). The two words mean the same but 'shocking up' was used in this locality. Two sheaves were picked up at the same time, one under each arm and stood upright, butts to the ground and ears pressed together. (See pictures pages 53-57).

Wheat and barley had 6-8 sheaves per shock, oats 10-12. The longer, softer straw stood together much better in larger quantities. The number of sheaves depended on how heavy the crop was. Shocking up prevented rain getting in while any straw that was still a little green, ripened. To put the corn into barns or stacks while straw is slightly green causes heating and a possible fire.

Shocking up is not as easy as it might seem and needs patience, the straw being quite slippery. I remember oats being difficult to erect due to the longer smooth straw.

We had a father and son working for us. The father was having trouble. Two sheaves were stood up. Two more were collected but the first pair had collapsed. He put four together, hoping for the best. No, it was not to be. When he returned with sheaves five and six, the four were flat and there were six more to find and they must all be standing firm. After much head-scratching, cap throwing and cursing, finally 12 sheaves were in a group. Working quickly, the old man, who had dealt with such tricky situations many times before, had all the sheaves standing. Heaving a sigh of relief he moved on to build another. Out of the corner of his eye, he saw his son, who had been teasing his father something rotten, saying "he's had it" and "couldn't do a proper job". What was that in the son's right hand? A large clod of dried earth, which he threw hitting the corn shock amidships like a torpedo, demolishing the whole lot.

The standing corn is a haven for a lot of wildlife. Sparrows attack the grain with gusto; that which is dropped is a tasty meal for field mice. Rabbits live on the greenery at the bottom. A red fox, perhaps with a late litter of inquisitive cubs, are hidden away, but not far from essential water. The vixen with her sharp hearing and acute sense of smell will move the family at the slightest hint of danger. The hedge will do nicely in an emergency. Then nearby, the vixen's next move is the adjoining wood which is plentiful in cover from giant oaks to splendid ash and smooth-barked hornbeam. The undergrowth of dense sharp brambles and bracken is now  beginning to turn yellow where it was once green. Nearby, the stream – fed by a fresh spring farther up – trickles its way over a stony bed, the water clear and cold. The foxes have found their new home.

The binder continues its work, now the amount left to cut is small. A grey squirrel beats a hasty retreat still carrying the chewed-off ear when just a moment ago he was sitting on his haunches enjoying a treat. The rabbits run deeper into the corn, reluctant to make a dash for freedom. This, I'm afraid, is their undoing because there is a gun waiting. Crouching low to the ground, the rabbit is safe as the machine passes over, cutting the corn, but this leaves the animal disorientated. You will have heard about the rabbit getting caught in the headlights. Same thing.

From my seat, on the binder I see the rabbit in the stubble. Quickly jumping down I am able to grab it, making sure that it is not a squirrel or a lurking rat. The rabbit is meat for my family.

We as a family of seven would consume as many as a dozen rabbits a week during war time. Mother would cook them in various ways including roasting, stews and pies. From the age of about eleven I undertook the task of preparing the rabbits for cooking.

Taught by my father, I quickly learned how to take their jackets (skin) off, joint them and place in salt water (to remove any blood left in the flesh) ready for cooking the following day.

Rabbit meat is very similar in texture and taste to that of chicken.

During the war years and after while food was still rationed, many rabbits were utilised by hotels and restaurants. Several rabbits would be cooked together with, say, one chicken, all the meat was served as chicken.

When any unripe straw has dried out, the crop is picked up and loaded onto wagons with pitchforks, butts pointing outwards, ears to the centre, with two more sheaves side by side lying centrally longways on the ears of the first loaded, to hold them in place. These 'tiers' or layers would be eight or nine high to complete a load. The corn is stored in barns and stacks to await threshing during the winter.

Badgers whilst naturally nocturnal can be seen in daylight. In times of very dry conditions, they will forage more due to the short supply of food. Youngsters like to sunbathe, sitting on the mound of now dry sandy soil which the adults had drawn out from their 'setts' in January, using their bear-like paws with curved claws, to make a new chamber in readiness for the birth of the cubs in February. Nesting materials consisting of dried grass and reeds are collected. The bedding is frequently changed. Old bedding is brought to the surface to dry and air. Badgers love the growing corn, some is eaten when the grain is soft and milky, but a field of near mature crop is an ideal playground. A clan of badgers can ruin a large area, flattening it by standing on their strong hind legs, pulling the straw down, eating a little. The whole family together enjoying themselves rolling and gambolling to such an extent that a 'crop circle' is formed, something akin to the pictures seen in the media.

About 25 years ago, a neighbour came to complain that our horses had got into his wheat field and made a mess. He was not at all happy. Bob and I went with him to investigate. There were no broken fences and no evidence that horses had entered the field. Our terriers were running through narrow tracks that the farmer said the horses had made. Bob and I looked at each other and the man and said, "Badgers". We led the farmer to the 'headland' (a narrow strip of land between crop and hedge), showing him the badger latrines.

Of course, he was full of apologies, saying that he had no idea that they caused this amount of damage. And if this was the case, no wonder the West Country folk were up in arms. Badgers had caused a vast amount of damage in the corn crop and caused TB in cattle, which is a problem to this day.

Then came the first combine harvesters which started to appear on the farms. Some larger estates purchased their own while smaller growers relied on local contractors.

Combines were small at first with the cut being a similar width to the binder. The corn was threshed within the machine, the straw came out at the back, the grain came down four shutes to one side to which bags were attached. Bags were tied by hand and dropped off to be collected later. This early machine, for obvious reasons, was known as a 'bagger combine'.

From these basic machines have come today's large monsters, gobbling up a 24ft wide strip in one swipe.

The combine collects the grain in an internal holding tank and then pours via an extended shute straight into an open grain trailer, tractor-pulled, running alongside in unison with the combine. The straw is still delivered as the earlier machines did. A chopper can be fitted to mulch the straw which is then ploughed back into the land.

Everything is the modern technology of such intensity that it is almost impossible for any faults to be repaired by the operator/driver.

# Charcoal Burning

Historically, charcoal burning has been continuous in the Weald of Kent since the Iron Age and any Charcoal Burner today should, with a degree of pride, cherish the fact of being part of one of the civilised world's oldest and continuous trades.

Julius Caesar noted iron production in the South East of England when he arrived in 54BC.

In hop drying, charcoal was used to start the fires in the oast houses because it ignited easily and would then help ignite the Welsh anthracite which was the main fuel in hop drying.

Charlie Light was a charcoal burner here in 1940-50s. He lived at Little Park Gate, Mill Pond Lane, off the Cranbrook Road. Interestingly the Mill Pond featured in his address was the site of a hammer mill used in iron production that was reliant on charcoal for the production of pig iron in the 1700s. Indeed much of England's cannon was the end product of Kent's iron industry.

Almost any hardwood was used; oak, ash, hornbeam, chestnut and hazel. The wood needed to be 'sare' (dry-seasoned) but not rotten.

The site on which the charcoal was burned was known as a Pit and had to be on level ground, the earth, with a good supply of water nearby, usually a pond. If the site was uneven the fire would not spread through the wood thoroughly.

Wood was cut into four-feet lengths. A pole about 8 feet long with cross pieces attached was placed in the centre. The lengths of wood were placed evenly around the pole.

*Stacking the wood to form the charcoal pit.*

*Covering the wood with straw to insulate the pit.*

*Lighting the fire from the top of the mound.*

*Tipping hot ashes in the top to start the fire.*

*Ashing up. Notice the second pit in the background as they always built two.*

*Cooling down towards the end of burning.*

*Opening up the pit after cooling, ready to bag up the charcoal.*

*An extraordinarily large piece of charcoal.*

The cross pieces held the wood in place. The wood was built up two lengths high, the top stack leaning slightly in towards the central pole. When completed it resembled the old-type beehive.

The wood was then covered with bracken, dead grass, straw, whichever was available, and covered with dust and/or ashes to keep it airtight. A fire was lit internally by placing easily combustible material around the central pole and pouring shovels of hot ash or coals into the top of the pit. Once alight the top of the pit was sealed off so that the fire just smouldered. Should fire break through, it was doused with buckets of water and ashed-up again.

The process took three days and nights to burn from the centre to the outside. When finished the fire was extinguished with water and left to cool.

The Charcoal Burner needed to be in attendance most of the time and usually slept in an improvised canvas tent. In later years he had the luxury of a van to sleep in.

When the charcoal was completely cold the ash covering was removed. If this was done too soon and it was still hot it could burst into flames as the air got to it.

Finally, it was put into hessian bags ready for use. The charcoal was made in the summertime because hop picking started usually the first week in September.

Charlie had the help of two of his sons, Charlie Jnr and Peter. One time, Peter was exploring a pile of unused timber when some gave way and he fell into a huge wasp's nest and had to be rescued by his dad. All had to take cover in their van.

There were usually a few 'brands' left. This is where the fire had not completely engulfed the wood, leaving a piece six to 10 inches long with a charred end. These were quickly gathered up and put to good use on the duck's nest fire.

All the charcoal made on our farm was used in the Oast House.

Much of the charcoal, burned elsewhere was sent off to London for use in smelting down iron ore, and during the war, ultimately to make munitions. Whole areas lost their ornamental iron railings during this period, taken from town parks and churchyards. Interestingly St Mildred's Church railings in Tenterden were taken and never restored, although the signs are still apparent. The concrete base still shows where the railings were cut off.

Historically charcoal was used in the making of gunpowder, discovered by the Chinese in the 9th century. Along with ingredients such as salt peter and sulphur, it could be said to have changed the world. There are many other uses as in Horticulture and Medicine.

The use of charcoal in the production of iron and steel manufacture declined on the discovery of the more versatile coke.

# Root Vegetables and Peas

Potatoes, turnips, swedes and mangold wurzels (a kind of beet similar in colour to a swede but with an elongated tuber, shaped a little bit like an upturned cone), were grown as winter feed for sheep and cattle. Of course, some of the potatoes, turnips and swedes were used for our consumption too.

Potatoes and mangold wurzels would rot if left in wet fields and needed to be lifted (dug up) and stored in Autumn.

Whereas today cold stores are used for this purpose, in my younger days the roots had to be clamped.

Usually, a fairly high spot of land was used or space dug into a bank. The selected place was lined with a thick layer of wheat straw, used because of its stiffness and is less absorbent, the root vegetables were piled onto the straw. If the clamp was on a flat piece of ground, the shape would become semi-circular to prevent any potatoes or wurzels falling off. Once all were in place the clamp was covered in straw with plenty of earth thrown on top to keep the straw in place and render the clamp watertight.

When the contents were needed in winter a small opening was made, the required amount   removed and then resealed.

Turnips and swedes were often left on their growing site. Sheep would be turned into the field to feed on them there.

Peas are sown in the Spring. The countryside is waking up after winter, buds and blossoms are bursting. The hawthorn leaf is showing in the hedges. The birds have had their Wedding Day (February 14th). Throughout the Autumn and Winter, the pigeons have crammed their crops full of acorns,

71

ivy berries and green stuff such as the tops (leaf) of the turnips and swedes, perhaps some clover and shoots of winter sown corn.

Now the birds need sustenance for the forthcoming breeding season. The peas have just been sown. There are always a few left uncovered, especially if the seed has been broadcast (sown by hand), the sower using a trug secured to the body by straps around neck and shoulders, with both hands scatters the seed over the ground, walking the field. Even after harrowing, not every seed was covered. Sometimes a thorn bush was used for this task. Cut off at ground level, a chain attached to the butt of the bush which a horse then pulled over the crop. The fine branches and twigs at the top of the bush were an ideal harrow.

Pigeons lay 2 eggs, then incubate them. After rearing the two squabs, they repeat the process, often using the same nest – a jumble of twigs in a hedge, tree or building – and will continue to breed well into Autumn in good weather.

Wood pigeons have a great liking for peas. Sitting on the branch of an overhanging oak tree, the birds see a few peas and drop down to feed. Returning to the tree, wiping its beak on the bark, it starts to coo in satisfaction. It seems to be saying "Tomfool, sow more peas".

# Hops

Hops are planted 6 feet apart, to form alleys in both directions, to allow a horse or tractor room to pull a plough or shim through to cultivate the soil, add manure and to 'ridge up', cover the plant, as you would earth up potatoes to protect growing tubers from light. Ridging up for hops was done late Autumn to safeguard the plant (hill) from hard frost and then opened up late February to access the plant for dressing, cutting away any dead plant and encouraging new shoots to grow. Hops grow on Bines as opposed to grapes growing on Vines. Whereas grape vines, although slightly woody and flaky in appearance, they are not unkindly to the touch, the young hop bines are fine but when mature, they become coarse and rough in texture, the purple coloured bines can scratch and tear skin, leaving red wheals and even cuts.

In the early days of hop growing, each plant was supported by one pole up which the hops climbed. This was known as pole work, no string was used. At hop picking time, men known as Pole Pullers would lift the poles from the ground and lay them across the bins.

Then came wirework – longer stouter poles were positioned at every other hill (known as wirework bats), a wire was fixed near the top. Looking up from beneath, one could see the silvery grey mesh-type 'roof' hung with hooks onto which the string is attached for the hops to grow up. On the ground, wire screw pegs are screwed in close to the poleless hill, to hold the string, with a nail used on the poles. Using a long light pole, (these were often hand-made on the farm), with a metal top for the string to run through, old bike handlebars were ideal for this purpose. The stringer (person applying the string) carrying a string bag with a strap either around neck or shoulders, containing a ball of coir hop string, walked fixing string on pegs at ground level and hooks above, putting four strings to each hill. Next, the strings at the plant needed to be 'banded in'. A string was tied around the supports to make about a 4" square, at approximately 5ft high, leaving a free passage for machinery and horses.

At strategic points around the outside of the hop garden, to create stability, extra large poles were erected and nailed to the overhead wire. Another wire ran from pole top to a large piece of wood buried deep into the ground. The three elements were called Anchor men, Anchor wire and Deadmen. Later on, iron stays replaced the deadmen.

The next stage is training the hops (twiddling). Two young bines are put to each string to which they cling and grow (opposite direction to runner beans). This process goes on throughout the spring months, repeatedly inspecting making sure no bines have fallen or crossed over to another string or hill. The hops should be 'over the top' by June 21st.

Now the hops had to be looked after for the 10-12 weeks. Like most other crops, they get diseases and parasites too – downy mildew, wilt and red spider.

The hop powdering machine, either horse or tractor pulled, a two-wheeled drum-like affair with two upward pointing funnels at the rear was towed through the alleys, blowing out white hop powder or bluestone as was necessary.

This operation had to take place on a still, quiet morning when the plants were still wet with dew. Often at the break of day. As time progressed sprays and insecticides injected into the plant were used. This meant that Grandfather, Dad and myself, no longer came home in either white or blue attire.

The hop plants come into (Burr) flower mid-July. During the next three weeks, it slowly develops into a small green

74

# The Cider Maker's Wife

^ *Hop Picker's Account Book* ^

< *Mr G Crouch transports his hops to Tenterden station from Goodshill Farm on the Cranbrook Road in the early 1920s. Photo courtesy of Tenterden & District Museum.*

*Grandad Tom Clarke, Bert Moon and me measuring hops 1954.*

*Tenterden has been involved in the hop trade for generations. A typical hop garden in about 1910. © Tenterden & District Museum*

*^ Christine, David and Joan in the hop garden with a friend.*

*Top left: Joan, myself, David and Christine on a load of hop pokes in late 1940s.*

*< Hopping. Christine centre with Mary and Shirley Bishop.*

hop, the actual fruit. Although it looks more flower-like than Burr. Another three weeks is needed for it to grow into a fully fledged hop. The tiny seed is contained within the green petal structure, not yet open. Hops must be picked before the seed falls.

August was preparation month for Hop picking.

The buildings in which pickers from London and Brighton were to live during the following month were scrubbed and whitewashed.

The hop pickers' huts were built of corrugated iron. They weren't that big either. More than tall enough for a person to stand upright and room to eat and sit, and on one side was made a bed built from wood, a platform-type bed standing a couple of feet off the floor. Clean straw was made available just before hopping each year and that was their bedding, although they did bring some other bedding with them and the families made these little huts into quite nice habitable places for their working holiday – which is how the Londoners looked upon it at that time.

*Mum hop picking.*     *My sister Joan in the hop garden.*

The cookhouse was brick-built and it had two large open fireplaces inside and they were fuelled mainly by wood. I suppose a bit of coal used to get nicked from time to time, but it was mainly faggots or small tops from any kind of hardwood, and this was the hoppers cooking and water heating fuel for 4-6 weeks. ( See faggot picture page 48).

A 20-ton truckload of Welsh Anthracite coal came into Tenterden station, to be off-loaded by hand and taken to the Oast at Pigeon Hoo by a lorry. The faggots, made when the chestnut was coppiced the previous winter, now completely 'sare' (dry) and browny-black, the binding hazel wisps now silvery white, are brought from the woods where they have been stacked around the trunk of an oak.

The bins are brought out of their resting place. Woodwork and cloths are inspected and renewed. Some bins are home-made with chestnut and some manufactured. Any small hole in a cloth was darned or patched with a sacking needle and coping string. Those bins who had seen years of work and had a rotting cloth, suddenly came alive again when a new vibrant yellow-orange garment was added, tacked on with a shiny new chestnut wood strip.

In the oast, the hair (horsehair matting) is checked for large holes. The hops lie on this during the drying process. The Press is oiled and greased. The yellowy hessian pokes into which the newly picked green hops are measured by the bushel are made ready. A tall light-coloured jute pocket is fixed into the press with a wooden hoop at floor level, with a webbing sling beneath for support during pressing, awaiting the first dried hops.

The hop drier and his mate prepare their bedding in the blue painted waggon body on the oast floor. Once picking starts there will be little rest or time off for them. They will live in the oast from Monday morning until pressing is finished the next Sunday mid-morning.

The oast gets a general spruce and check-up from the large sliding door, the sixteen open-brick fireplaces (eight fires to each kiln), steps and gantries. The cowl has had two coats of paint and is now brilliant white, waiting for the wind to change to move it, to show itself off even more. There are two loose tiles quite high up on the roundel that need fixing. Dad, with the aid of one of the younger workers, Peter, erect two ladders, strapped one above the other. (Elf) Health & Safety would not permit this method today. Scaffolding would be necessary. Dad climbs the ladder, followed by Peter, their hob-nailed boots clinging to the wooden rungs. Peter hands Dad tools and materials when needed, but has to descend for more. Peter does not like the height of the work, and calls out; "Leo, I would rather be up a ladder down a well, than up here". When wells dried up, ladders were lowered into the well for maintenance and the retrieval of any buckets and the like that had previously been dropped or had fallen off the hooked chain.

September is here. The pickers have arrived and settled into their huts. Suddenly everything springs into life, blue smoke rises from the cookhouse chimney. Mothers are yelling at their kids to bring in more faggots but keep away from the fire, where black pots and kettles bubble noisily. Up go the washing lines, tied from hut to cookhouse to telegraph pole in the thorny hedge. An array of garments of all colours and sizes, towels and nappies (non-disposable), made from terry towelling, adorn the lines held in place by the wooden pegs, often made by local gypsies, using two pieces of lightweight wood bound at the top by a tin ferrule (cut from any old tin can). Radios are blaring out Housewives Choice or Family Favourites on Sunday.

While the pickers were sorting themselves out, the bins were placed in the hop alleys, the growing hop either side of bins so that there were four hills to be picked. When this was achieved, the bin was moved manually by the pickers to the next 'move' and so on, until that set was completed.

On the first day of picking, pickers were allotted half or a whole bin, depending on the number and the ability of workers. The bins were then put into 'sets', two bins to the set e.g. 20 bins = 10 sets. Whichever bin completed their row first would turn into their partner's row until both rows were picked. This method kept continuity and the hop garden tidy and accessible to collect the filled pokes after measuring.

Lots were drawn at the beginning of picking to prevent arguments as to who was to pick where. Small hazel sticks with notches cut into them were used for this purpose. When all was ready, the order "All to work", was given. The pickers then received a Hop Pickers Account Book in which was recorded the number of bushels picked each day. Twice a day the measure man would visit each bin, using a 1-bushel wicker measuring basket and remove the picked hops from the bin into a hop poke, made of yellow/orange hessian. Each poke held 10 bushels. The measure man carried an account book too. Both picker and farmer then had a record of picked hops. (Picture: Hop Pickers Account Book page 75).

If any bins of hops were 'dirty' – containing too much leaf or roughly picked – they would not be measured until the picker had cleaned the hops to the correct standard.

Forty pokes (400 bushels) was required for an 'oasting' – the amount of hops that could be dried at one time, in one kiln. Drying time was approximately 8 hours. Pigeon Hoo was a 2-kiln oast. Over the course of 24 hours 1200 bushels were dried. In the early days, horse and cart and later lorry or tractor and trailer collected the pokes from the hop garden and transported them to the oast for drying.

The pickers were paid per bushel. The rate/price varied from 6d, six old pence (2½ new pence) to 1/- one shilling

(5 pence) per bushel. If the hops were small, pickers would complain. "They are small Sir", hoping for a higher price. Also if the hops were 'housy' – being a lot of large leaf or course bine which meant the actual hop was 'housed in'– and it was difficult for fingers to reach the hop, more money was demanded.

By and large, the Londoners were a high-spirited people. The fact that they had lived through the war, the blitz and doodlebugs had not dampened their spirits one bit. They were always ready for a laugh.

During picking some of the women were seen heading for the make-shift toilets, others would yell out "We know where you're going", followed by shrieks of laughter. At weekends they would take a sub (money from their account) for shopping, reserving some for their Saturday night 'knees-up' at one of the local pubs. Rolling home after closing time belting out the likes of 'My old man said follow the van' and 'Roll out the Barrel.' In inclement weather conditions in the hop garden, they would have a sing-song, keeping their spirits up.

Teenagers were lively too. One such girl frequented the oast until she made a nuisance of herself and annoyed the oast workers at pressing time.

The hop pockets were required to be numbered and dated with the year, using a metal stencil and black boot polish. This girl needed to be taught a lesson. A ladder extended from the ground floor to the press floor. One of the hands, armed with boot polish and brush descended halfway down the ladder while the other two chased the girl to the top of the ladder. She had no option but to climb down. As she did so, she was blackened with boot polish from her ankles to her bottom.

When hop-picking was finished the pockets of hops were transported by lorry to Borough Market in London, the home of the Hops Marketing Board to which several dealers called Hop Factors belonged. My Grandfather Tom Clarke used W.H & H Le May who were Hop Factors in Borough High Street, Southwark. These people dealt with the sales of English hops all over the world. In late October/November, the hop samples were taken by cutting a small square from the side of the pocket and removing a chunk of the tightly pressed dry hops. Each farmer was invited up to London to look at the samples in front of the dealers when the price of the crop would be determined after close examination. The price was made on hop quality, eg properly dried containing few leaves and no bine. Every time London was visited, (rare) a West End show was attended before coming home.

The oast at Pigeon Hoo was the only oast where all the hops were dried. Pigeon Hoo was purchased some years before, in the late 1920s, just for the purpose of drying the hops. The house was sold off but three fields were made into hop gardens and the one nearest the oast housed the hopper huts for the Londoners and their cookhouse. There was no mains water supply and once again the water came from a well on the edge of Pigeon Hoo house which was about two fields away. It must have been 150 yards or more. Of course, everything had to be bucketed back from the well to the cookhouse and for washing.

Pigeon Hoo lies in Preston Lane which runs from the Woodchurch Road through to the Appledore Road. It's about halfway down from Woodchurch Road on the right, almost opposite The Dandy. The Dandy belonged to Sir Reginald Hooper who was managing director of Schweppes.

In early springtime, end of February, early March, everything needed to be done quickly and labour was sometimes short. The main job at that time was dressing the hops which meant trimming the hill. The hill is the hop plant and it needs

83

to be trimmed each year to cut away any dead roots and to get it back into shape and size for the coming growth.

Every so often gypsies would be taken in, just to do the dressing, although at times they didn't particularly make a good job of it. At one point, there were about three families called in to do the job and they started fighting among themselves. A local resident called the Police because there was such a schmozzle going on. A police car and constables arrived and pulled up under the hedge, waited for them to have their fight and sort themselves out, and then they just disappeared again. They were always frightened of the gypsies because if they decided to intervene in the fight, then the whole lot would turn around and set about the police, so they thought, better safe than sorry.

Pickers also came up from Brighton and these were based at Heronden. They were housed in the old cowshed that had been scrubbed out and whitewashed, so they were in comparative luxury to those in the huts. Also, we had local pickers and they were collected up in the farm lorry and brought to Heronden from Tenterden town. Then all three farms would be picking at once, Heronden, Pigeon Hoo and Rolvenden, but if one farm got behind, pickers were brought in from one of the other farms. A Maidstone & District single-decker bus would be hired to bring them and the locals to wherever they were needed. Dad's brother Harry was Foreman/Manager for the bus company for several years.

# Modern Day Hop Farming

Hop farming, like most other types of farming, underwent changes.

The early days of wirework saw men on stilts who walked the hop gardens repairing wires and putting on hooks, adding staples at the pole tops, replacing a loose bine that had become separated from the string. Later on, poles with attachments were used for stringing and other tasks and replaced the stilts men.

Tractors replaced the horses. Machinery such as the hop powdering machine, were improved. Next came the most radical change, the hop picking machine. Buildings were adapted or custom built to house this large piece of equipment. This meant that where a machine existed, hand pickers were no longer required. The bustle and camaraderie of the hop garden was extinct.

Some manual labour, of course, was still needed – tractor drivers and a man for the 'crows nest' (a metal scaffold-like platform, fitted to the back of the specially made high-sided trailers). Loading the trailers was a three-man operation. The first walked the alleys cutting the bines at the banding-in string. Secondly, the crows nest man cut the hops at the overhead wires. Hops dropped into the trailer where a third person pulled the tail ends between two supports. At least three tractors and trailers were needed to ensure a continual supply of hops to the picking machine. Two people were required to remove the bines from the trailer and on to the conveyor chains which transported the hops to the picker. The first person pushed the bine ends into the conveyor cups, the second made sure bines were not tangled, for efficient and clean picking. Four more workers, usually women, were leaf pickers, discarding large leaves and other rubbish. The hops ended up in pokes as they did when being measured after hand picking. The last person to measure the hops to the best of my knowledge is Neil Ridley from Smarden in 1971. (See photo below).

Solid fuel fires changed to fan assisted diesel oil burners.

Hop growing declined when lager beer was imported into this country. Lager was a sweeter beer and did not require hops for the bitter taste. By the end of the 20th Century, many Oasts had been converted into dwellings, but they still retain their distinctive shape and cowls.

In recent years several small breweries have sprung up. Hops are needed again. Growers are planting new gardens.

New varieties of hop have been bred and introduced. Some, dwarf-like plants growing only about 10 feet high and grown on trelliswork, thus allowing them to be harvested on-site by machinery.

*The Last Measure - Neil Ridley 1971 measuring hops with his wife Rosemary Graham booking in for the last year of hand picking for V H Millen & Son at Wagstaff Farm (his uncle's farm) Biddenden.*

# The Railway

The railway's first section ran from Robertsbridge Junction through Bodiam, Northiam, Wittersham Road to Rolvenden and passed through Heronden land.

It was named the Rother Valley Railway as the track ran alongside the River Rother for some way and crossed part of the Rother Levels at Northiam. This stretch was constructed in the mid to late 1800s.

A group of corrugated dwellings known locally as Tin Town was built on Rolvenden Hill to house the construction workers. Tin Town has been massively redeveloped over the years to form a smart housing complex called The Bungalows.

There were two large 'Sand Holes' on Heronden which I was told as a child had been dug out for the sand to be used in the line construction.

The hole on Mensden Bank being about 100 yards from the track itself. The other on the south side of Foxbury Wood was a little further distant. Grass grew around the perimeter of the holes but the sand was still visible in the basin and steep sides. Rabbits burrowed into the soft yellow sand. The sand afforded dry, warm but sometimes unstable homes for the grey furry creatures.

Here at Little Halden Place (where I now live), bordering the Cranbrook Road, about ¼ mile from the Cranbrook Road crossing, is another large, deep area that I assume was excavated for the building of the railway track. This area is rich in sand and sandstone. Imagine two horses with a cart, laden with sand, toiling up the steep climb to the track.

The line reached Tenterden in 1900. About five years later, the railway was extended to Headcorn where it linked up with the mainline trains, as did Robertsbridge in East Sussex. The line was then renamed the Kent and East Sussex Railway. It was also known as the 'Farmer's Line' due to the amount of agricultural produce, supplies, equipment and livestock it transported. Also it brought the annual hop pickers from Brighton and London, and believe it or not, in the Spring, bunched primroses.

My mother would take us children into the woods to pick the fresh primrose flowers into open baskets to prevent them being crushed, collecting as many as possible. The blooms were then divided into bunches of between 17 and 20 blooms, surrounded by carefully picked, evenly sized leaves and bound with fine string. Next, they were put into water to ensure they were fully freshened before being carefully packed into cardboard boxes lined with soft paper between the layers. The boxes were put on the London train at Tenterden Station for transporting to Covent Garden market for sale in the City florists. I think they were sold for about 6d (six old pence) per bunch for which payment was received by post later.

As many, if not more, goods trains ran as did passenger services. When passenger services ceased in 1954-55, private transport had to be arranged to bring the hoppers from Brighton and to collect the Londoners from Headcorn.

Roy Wickens from Rolvenden was the last carrier to do the Brighton run in 1959.

The increasing use of road transport saw even more decline in the small lines.

Dr Beeching then axed many small lines in 1960. In the summer of the following year, 1961, I remember standing near to the line on Mensden Bank with my family to see,

# The Cider Maker's Wife

*The Terrier Loco and carriages going past Little Halden Place Farm*

© K.E.S.R  www.kesr.org.uk

as was then thought, the last ever train to pass through Heronden. An engine front and back, passengers with flags flying from windows. A spectacular sight.

The track from Tenterden to Headcorn was taken up, but there is today still evidence of the line. In St. Michaels, Tenterden, there is the cutting and tunnel under Shoreham Lane. In Biddenden Road and North Street, Biddenden still stands the original station buildings being put to good use.

This was not to be the end of K.E.S.R. Although the track from Tenterden to Robertsbridge fell into disrepair, it was never taken up. In the 1970s work began to repair and reconstruct the track. With the help of a band of volunteer enthusiasts, the railway re-opened in 1974. The train now runs the 10½ miles from Tenterden to Bodiam. Plans are in place to hopefully reach Robertsbridge again.

The K.E.S.R. is once again a going concern and a huge tourist attraction.

Purchasing Little Halden Farm in 2015 and seeing the trains in action again, re-kindled all my forgotten memories. I had seen trains running since a toddler, most days, until its closure. Sometimes right up close, with sheep penned near the line or when repairing fences.

Now I hear again the whistle as trains announce their presence. From the farmyard, looking west towards Rolvenden, I see the smoke billowing up beyond the treetops. In winter the smoke creeps through the bare trees. The train pulls out of Rolvenden Station with a belch of black smoke and a hiss of steam as it approaches the steep incline towards Cranbrook Road. Nostalgia kicks in. I have to stand and watch as the train comes into view, pulling five carriages. Struggling with the carriage weight and the incline... "I-think-I-can, I-think-I-can"... the loco puffs out. As the terrain levels out and speed increases so does the sound... 'I-think-I-can, I-think-I-can'.

On the return journey from Tenterden to Rolvenden, it is plain sailing, so to speak, it glides almost silent on its way with a quiet 'tiddi-tat, tiddi-tat' over the tracks.

The railway featured strongly in the family's lives without intrusion, as the track bordered our land to the south-west.

The family even told the time by the occasional engine. I remember the train leaving Rolvenden Station at 9.45am and 4.50pm for Robertsbridge, this knowledge being imperative since often we had to move livestock across the track; indeed one such tragic mistiming cost the lives of a number of sheep.

The railwaymen used a little bogey – also known as a pump trolley – for working along their section of track, the sort of thing we've seen in the old movies. This was their means of moving along for maintenance, sorting damaged sleepers, cleats and so forth. They had a little shed for inclement weather and for breaks in their work; a means of cooking and making hot drinks. It was comprised of wood and corrugated iron sheets with a wood stove in the corner.

My brother David had had one or two run-ins with these workers and one day resolved to get even with them. He noticed that the chimney pot was held on only by gravity; indeed the whole assembly was not physically connected, just a wide collar that fitted over the first section, as was often the case.

With this piece of knowledge, David waited for them to be away at their work, removed the top sections of the chimney, stuffed a wet old hessian sack down the pipe and restored the pieces he had removed. Of course, they came back ready for some tea, lit the fire and were soon choking from the smoke. David got away with this a couple of times before they deigned to mend the chimney so it could not be tampered with; at which stage an unconditional truce developed.

Not everyone can flag down a train and hop into it merely with a signal to the engine driver, but in those days this was the case for me and the family. We never went to the station, we walked across the fields, stopped the train along the tracks, and got on. The line follows the route of the Newmill Channel and crosses it less than 250 yards from Herondon Farm itself.

There are a number of footbridges and track crossings in this short section of line and visits to Battle Market often resulted in Grandfather getting on a train with the animals purchased, and then being off-loaded from the cattle wagons at one of these points.

The railway line itself was targeted by the Luftwaffe during the war and was liberally bombed by incendiaries, but as railway engineers often throw out hot clinker, the sight of a burning embankment troubled no one.

During the war the line carried materials to improve local aerodromes, including Headcorn and Smarden.

We had a large sheep pen right close to the railway line because it was convenient when the sheep were either in the marsh or up on the banks. Most of the drivers knew us and they would either wave at us as they passed by or whistle.

# The War

The war did have its effect upon the residents of Heronden for whereas children from this region were being sent in large numbers off to safer areas with their labelled clothes and cardboard gas mask cases, Heronden boasted a very large cellar deemed by the powers-that-be to be sufficient protection for the whole family.

Many an air raid warning sent the family scurrying to sleep on makeshift beds in the cellar. It did not, however, have a suitable escape route and Father had to knock a hole through the wall at ground level so that we could get out if necessary, and this also provided ventilation. Of course, there was no light, we had to use candles and paraffin lamps.

We could hear the siren go off in Golden Square in Tenterden. It used to give the all-clear as well. The family spent ever so many nights in the cellar. We kids thought that it was fun.

Interestingly, the government approved the production of the Anderson shelter before Britain declared that a state of war existed in September of 1939. Having the cellar, an Anderson shelter was not necessary for us.

The war had been going on for some years before the Germans invented the flying bomb - or Doodlebug as the Londoners named it. The chances of Heronden being hit by one of these speculatively aimed aircraft was deemed very low as sitting on 400 acres of farmland and being nowhere near London made for a great feeling of security. However, the farm was on the direct route to London.

One afternoon, about 5 pm in July of 1944, the family, that's Grandfather Tom Clarke, my mum, dad, toddler Joan and I had almost finished our tea when a plane was heard firing, along with the distinctive engine sound of a Doodlebug. It is said they had a throbbing sound like a heavy motorcycle.

Grandfather Tom was relaxing on the sofa by the window and my little sister Joan had wandered outside.

Mum told Dad to go out and find Joan, at the same time instructing me to get under the very robust kitchen table. By now two aircraft could be heard accompanied by the rattle of gunfire.

My mother, very concerned for her husband and daughter Joan went outside to find them. Not wanting to be left alone under the kitchen table I ran outside too.

Grandfather had by now got up from the sofa where he was resting and joined everyone outside, perhaps not wanting to miss out on the action. As he stood by the back door, cigarette packet and matches in his hand with the thought of having a smoke, and perhaps a little bleary-eyed from his nap, there was an enormous explosion, as the Doodlebug crashed into the field of standing corn about 300 yards away.

The force of the blast blew the windows out, leaving glass at Grandfather's feet; his cigarettes were gone, snatched from his hands. On returning to the living room we had just vacated, we found it completely wrecked. The sofa where Grandfather had been relaxing only moments before was covered with glass from the windows. The large Aladdin paraffin lamp had crashed onto the kitchen table, covering it in glass and paraffin. Everything was ruined.

Upstairs, the skylight in the roof had caved in, blocking the staircase and most of the ceilings were on the beds.

Meanwhile, the field where the Doodlebug had landed was on fire, very quickly destroying two acres of ripe grain.

The fire brigade came to put the corn out and they also helped us clear the debris off the stairs to help us to get up to the bedrooms.

Earlier in the war, a number of oil bombs (so-called) had been jettisoned by German bombers in a hurry to get home, leaving huge craters that were visible for years after.

Some while after the bombs had been jettisoned across the farm, Dad was out lookering one summer morning, when nearing home, he was walking alongside the Shaw (a narrow strip of woodland) when he heard a methodical 'tick, tick, tick'. Fearing that the sound was coming from a time bomb – as everyone had the 'jitters' at this time – not knowing what to expect, his first instincts were to run.

Dad was a member of the Home Guard. He was issued with a rifle and a bayonet attachment, which was kept in the house. When he was on duty the assembly point was the Drill Hall in Church Road, now St. Mildred's Hall.

He decided to investigate, perhaps, in case there were more close by. Carefully he entered the wood, the ground sloped down to the centre to a little ditch. The undergrowth was thick and green. The ticking became louder as he approached. With trembling hands, he began to pull apart the foliage which he expected to reveal a metallic canister-like object. Peeping through the leaves, to his surprise and utter relief, he saw at the water's edge, a song thrush, snail in beak, tapping it on a large stone to crack the shell.

# The War Prisoner

A German prisoner of war was employed as one of the Plate Layers (track maintenance) by the K.E.S.R. Working regularly on the track which ran through Heronden Farm, he saw my family going about our work, I and sometimes my sister Joan were with our parents and grandfather.

In his spare time – I never knew his name – he collected scraps of wood. From this, he hand-carved a toy of four chickens standing on a plate-like base. There were strings attached to each bird's head threaded through the base to a tassel-like object. When held by the base handle and rotated, the chicken's heads would bob up and down. Each bird was etched with red-hot wire to create feathers and combs and the grain on which they were apparently feeding. He gave this handmade toy to my sister and I and I still have it to this day.

*Chicken toy made by a German prisoner of war.*

*'Digging for Victory'. An illustration by Trevor Mitchell showing farmer and Land Army girls digging potatoes. www.trevormitchellartist.com ©.*

# Water

Heronden was very basic and probably a typical farmhouse as I remember it in the early 1940s. There was just a soak-away, no mains drainage or even a septic tank or cesspit. There was no gas or electricity. Lighting was by paraffin lamps, cooking by one of those wonderful black ranges fed either by coke or wood. There was, however, one concession to modernity for the times, and that was a hand pump for water over the large salt-glazed sink. This pump drew from a deep well of spring water and saved the chore of carrying pails whenever it was needed. That is not to say the well didn't run dry in some summers, as did the pond beside the house - because they did - and despite the other catchment arrangements, roof water and the like, there would come the occasions when water had to be carried from a good spring on the lower levels of the marsh, just west of the railway tracks.

This was a long carry back to the house and the use of a shaped wooden yoke, medieval in concept but practical, enabled two pails to be carried back up the hill.

Outside, there were two large deep ponds situated close to the buildings and not far from the house itself. Each pond had a brickwork walk-in; this was to allow the cart horses to walk down to drink from the pond without getting stuck. Horses' hooves being uncloven act like suction pads in mud and without this facility, they could have become trapped.

Pond water was used for all the yarded cattle in winter times. Using metal buckets two at a time the water was carried to the stock twice a day. Often in the mornings, they had drunk all the water from the previous day's watering. They could drink faster than Dad and I could carry it. Eventually, we caught up with their demands. One animal could drink 10 gallons a day.

Fortunately, yarded animals were few in the summer.

Those with any knowledge of the husbandry of animals will appreciate the value of a good water supply. In the summer the stock on the marsh had access to the marsh ditches which were part of the water meadow husbandry where the flow was regulated by culverts and a series of adjustable barriers.

Water from the ponds was used for the poultry and gardens, but not for human consumption. All livestock needed this very labour-intensive provision.

In times of shortage not a drop of water was wasted. Washing-up water was used to flush the toilets or be used in the garden, especially to kill Dolphin (black fly) infestations on the broad beans with an old bike pump acting as a spray gun when the beans were in flower.

The buildings at home consisted of a large pole barn known as the Wagon Lodge which is what it was built for; a large brick stable; a very large old Kent barn and then buildings for a cowshed and five loose boxes, all adjoined in a U-shape. They were all brick-built with slate roofs. On one end of the cowshed was a feed room and next to that a wooden granary.

# Heronden Farm Cottages

There were seven cottages belonging to Heronden Farm. Five on the Old House part and two on New House. The two farms consisted of roughly 200 acres each and were run as one unit. The three cottages near to Heronden Old House were the original farmhouse that had been extended at the western end to make three cottages. Water was of course from a well. There were outside toilets which had to be emptied manually. The contents were usually buried deep in a garden corner.

These three cottages were last inhabited in 1962. When the last family moved out, they were given a council house. The local council insisted that parts of the tile roofs be removed to prevent any further occupation. In the 1970s they were subject to vandalism by some local youths who took no notice of my father chasing them off.

About this time, Grandfather who was then 85 years old, sold, (apart for the farmhouse and a few acres,) the rest of the farm to John Leroy (owner of Leroy Air Tours) who also owned the neighbouring Morghew Estate.

With an extraordinary nasty twist, a new Town Council decided that the old cottages should be preserved, but not on their original site where they were still standing.

There then ensued arguments as to where they should be rebuilt. Eventually, a piece of land on Plummer Farm, adjoining West View Hospital was chosen. Plummer Farm had previously been owned by the De Kraft family, the margarine company, as did Heronden Hall and the Lodge Gate opposite the William Caxton pub.

HERONDEN FARM
TENTERDEN

THURSDAY 24th
SEPTEMBER 1970

at 10.30 a.m.

W & B
hobbs

165 SHEEP
30 CATTLE
TRACTORS IMPLEMENTS AND
FARM EQUIPMENT

Auctioneers W. & B. Hobbs, 32 Bank Street,
Ashford, Kent. (Tel: 22222).

The other two cottages on Old Heronden were situated on Mensden Bank, about half a mile from our farmhouse. They were remote and isolated. Each had a good sized garden with a high, mostly thorn hedge, which encircled both gardens which were stocked with fruit trees. There was a large pond on the outskirts. The last inhabitants here were Mr and Mrs Bill Collins. Bill was a cobbler (shoe repairer) for Bert Swaine. Bert's grandson, David, closed their shop in March of this year 2017. Bill's wife used to help my mother in the house.

They moved out of Mensden Cottages in the early part of the war into the west end of the aforementioned cottages, mainly for safety. They used to spend some nights in the cellar with us. The two cottages were later demolished as nobody wanted to live so far out.

The two cottages on the New House part of the farm also met their end via the council. A local agricultural contractor with a young family went bankrupt and was homeless. One of the two cottages was empty. The then Town Clerk persuaded Grandfather to allow this family occupation.

Grandfather's generosity and hospitality were repaid by the occupant contaminating the water in the well and rendering the property to condemnation.

My future father-in-law, Old Bob Luck bought the New House land in 1959. He demolished the cottages in the 1960s.

Although the cottages were basic two-up two-down affairs, they were well built and stood the test of time.

Farm cottages were normally 'tied' cottages. In other words, the cottage went with the employee's job. If the worker lost his employment it meant he lost his home too. In the 1940s and 1950s, there were no CVs or written references to be had, only word of mouth between employers. If a worker got the sack it was usually a week's notice. No verbal and written warnings as today. Instant dismissal was just that.

There were a few sayings regarding the loss of work:

1 week's notice - *the sack.*

Instant dismissal - *got the sack and the string to tie it up with.*

A worker receiving the D.C.M - *Don't come Monday.*

The following incident occurred on a local farm in the 1950s:

As a farmer paid his workforce on Friday he announced to one, "Charlie you're sacked".

"Oh", said Charlie, shocked, then after a pause, "Does that mean I can work where I like?"

"Indeed it does", replied the farmer. "Thank you, sir, " said Charlie.

On Monday morning, Charlie arrived for work as usual. "I thought I sacked you, Charlie," the farmer remarked. "Yes sir, you did," Charlie answered, "but you said that meant I could work where I like" and with a smile continued, "I quite like working here!".

# Animals

I was introduced to farm life at an early age. My mother used to push me round in my pram to go ferreting.

Carthorses did all the farm work right up to the latter years of the war and just after when Grandfather bought a brand new Standard Fordson. Some of my earliest memories are of being carried on my father's back while I led the horse to and fro. We used to take wagon loads of hay down onto the bank to feed the bullocks in the wintertime, leave the wagon there, bring the horse back alone and then take another load down and fetch the empty wagon back as necessary. The bullocks ate the hay off the wagon.

My grandfather bought a new horse, a Suffolk Punch called Dolly, at Maidstone Market, where he persuaded or paid a lad to ride it home. The young lad rode this horse bareback (notwithstanding the fact he was a stranger to the animal) from Maidstone Market all the way to Heronden Farm, a distance of nearly 20 miles, counting the little roads and tracks he may have taken. Then, having delivered his charge, he was given refreshment and rest before walking across the marsh, crossing the Newmill Channel at Cradle Bridge to get to his home in Rolvenden. Not a bad day's work.

The Suffolk Punch draught horse nearly went into extinction in the war years. It is a very famous breed of horse, records date back to the 16th century. It is a broad well-muscled horse, always chestnut-red in colour and used to be referred to as the Suffolk Sorrel. The height varies from 16 to 17.2 hands high. Never to be confused with the Shire horses by virtue of never having feathered fetlocks.

Dolly the Suffolk Punch became redundant after the purchase of the tractor in early 1947. She was turned out to grass on the marsh.

In early April 1948, my youngest sister Christine was born and Mother was still in the nursing home. Mothers and babies were kept in for much longer than they are today. Even in the 1960s mothers spent 14 days in with the birth of the first child and 10 days for any subsequent children.

A buyer was sought for the horse. She was too young to waste. A potential buyer arrived at the farm to look at her at an inconvenient time. Grandfather was out. Father was looking after myself nine years, Joan five years and David barely two years. So, who got the job of introducing the buyer to the horse? Me.

Our cart horses were eventually replaced for the heaviest of tasks by a new Standard Fordson tractor, bought at Ken Jarvis's garage in St Michaels. It had big iron wheels to cope with the soft ground but could not replace the horse when it came to the narrow hop rows at Pigeon Hoo and elsewhere.

Tractors were later adapted so that they could be made narrower by turning the back wheels inside out and they were able to work in the hops.

When I was sixteen Grandfather said, "If I go out and buy a Fergie tractor, will you drive it?" I'd been used to the Standard Fordson, even repairing it, taking out and cleaning the plugs, putting them back together and getting it going, so I replied, "Yes, Grandad, I'll drive your tractor." It was a narrow tractor to work in the hops.

The tractor was duly delivered one evening, I got on it and in the bottom gear, it felt like I was doing about 30mph. I'd been told that I was going to be shimming the hops the next day, but I said to Dad, "I can't do this, I can't get used to the tractor by tomorrow," to which he replied, "Alright gal, I'll do it".

*A pair of Suffolk Punch horses ploughing.*

*Standard Fordson tractor with spade lugs.*　　　　　　© *Geoff Partner*

*This is a T20 narrow hop conversion 'Little Grey Fergie' tractor with a Perkins three-cylinder engine. On the back is a Howard rotovator. The picture is taken in an old-style hop garden with pole-work and strings. Photo courtesy of South East Farmer.*

I never did any hop work with the tractor but I did all the other work. I was second tractor driver after my dad! As I got older I took more of it on. I used to do all the mowing and all the hay turning and spreading artificial fertiliser which was in 1cwt (55 kilos) bags. I needed to pick these up from ground level to empty into the spreader.

On another occasion, a replacement house suckler cow was needed. As Mr McConkey who rented Morghew at the time was selling up, an Ayrshire cow called Milly was purchased and driven back to Heronden across three fields.

Next morning she was turned out with the other animals, but when the cows were to be brought in for milking in the afternoon she was nowhere to be seen. Then came a phone call saying that Milly had returned home, jumping gates and hedges stag-like. She was brought back and left in the cowshed for a couple of days but the same thing happened as soon as she was turned free. Dad came in, saying, "That old sod's gone again". Eventually, she did settle down when she realised that the rest of the Morghew herd was gone. I'm told that when I saw Milly I would shout at her, "Old sod. Old sod!"

## Sheep

Before I was of school age I helped my Father with the sheep. In the summertime when they had to be brought into the pen every day, I was seated in the corner, so I could see above the sheep, where I was safe and would not fall in amongst them and I soon learned to pick out a sheep that had got the fly.

Later on, I was expected to do my share with the sheep, especially when it came to blowfly treatment.

Blowfly or Green bottle (Lucilia sericata) attacks the sheep between March and November when the conditions, warm and mild, are right for them. They lay their eggs anywhere on the animal but are mostly attracted to the areas that are moist. Sheep that are not regularly 'dagged' of the tangled mud or faeces clumps are most vulnerable. Flocks that are not wormed or are put out onto new pasture are often scoured and their moist rear ends are a prime attraction for the blowfly.

There are several indications of the fly, either it has got a dirty stained bottom or is wiggling its tail or trying to bite its rear end. The blowfly lays its eggs in the wool and the maggots then hatch out and they are very soon into the sheep itself, if not treated. The wool around the affected area was trimmed off with a pair of hand shears. The wool roundabout was soaked in a solution of Jeyes fluid. If there were any sore patches on the sheep they were treated with ordinary cart grease. In those times, cart grease didn't have any detergents in it like the modern-day grease.

Of course these days there are many chemical sprays, pour-on's and dips.

It was and still is against the law to let these animals suffer from blowfly attacks. The treatment was messy and the stench of affected ewes almost unbearable, but as a farmer's daughter, I was there to do all that I was capable of.

Of course, I was not alone as my younger brother David was given to the same curiosity and need to be involved. Despite his lesser years, he would sit on the hurdle in the lambing shed to watch.

On one occasion my father was struggling to relieve a ewe of her lamb. When after a little difficulty the lamb was drawn away and rubbed down with a handful of straw, Father straightened up to ease his back and looked at David whose face was a picture of puzzlement. After a short pause, David said, "Is that, er, that sheep's lamb, Dad?"

"Yes, it is," replied Father.

After a further pause, David said, "Well, how did it get in there then?"

Sheep, goats and the like, that originate from hard rocky landscapes rarely suffer from foot problems, but this genre of animal has been adapted over time to live on the softer ground. As is the case with the Romney Marsh sheep or other sheep subject to the low-lying soft ground. The result is that the hooves are not worn down and rot can develop in the cloven part of the two digits they walk on.

*Bessie and sheep at Crit Hall, Benenden. >*

# Sheep dipping

It was required by law that sheep must be dipped twice within two months. The first dip would be done shortly after shearing, because a sheep with a saturated full fleece would have difficulty rising from the dip, causing stress etc. Shearing usually takes place in June, so the second dip would be in August.

The local Police sergeant had to be notified, who in turn, would send a constable to oversee the operation. Farmers faced a fine for non-notification and non-compliance with the rules.

Each animal had to be totally immersed in a prescribed chemical (a yellow-orange powder made by a firm called Coopers) of correct strength.

A large bath-like receptacle called a tun was dug into the earth so that the rim was level with the ground, filled with water and the correct amount of dip added.

Each sheep was lowered into the tun, hind end first and then pushed under with a special wooden crook, turned, then guided up the elevated step onto the draining pen where it was given time to shake before returning to the flock. The residual chemical drained back into the tun.

Regulations did get more stringent as to the protection of, not only the operator but the possible contamination of groundwater and springs by the careless disposal of the used dip chemicals. Sheep dipping was finally stopped by the Ministry and replaced by spraying.

Historically, when farms were sold, they changed hands in accordance with the planting and growth of crops: Lady

Day 25th March and at Michaelmas 24th September.

All the farm stock was sold by auction on the farm. Livestock was penned according to age, sex, breed and colour. This procedure was important especially for cattle, to produce a 'matching bunch'. Young heifers, 8-9-month-old calves, coming into their first heat/season are known as Bulling heifers and were sought after. Cattle were mostly of red Sussex and the dual purpose Shorthorn whose colouring was normally strawberry roan.

Sheep were the native Kent, now known as Romneys and the more compact close-wooled Southdown. Often the two breeds were crossed and called half-breeds. Also, some black-faced Suffolks were seen and the roman-nosed Border Leicester.

Deadstock included all the farm's machinery, hand tools, hardware and often household items. All the lots were laid out in rows in a field with the auctioneer walking on one side of the rows and bidders on the other, for visibility.

At Michaelmas 1961, Potts Farm, Chennel Park Road had been sold as Mr and Mrs Care had retired. I attended the auction of the farm stock on the farm with my grandfather. Grandfather bought a pen of 25 ewes.

The movement of animals in the 1960s had nothing like the same restrictions as today.

Transport for the job was available for short distances, but it was not considered necessary for the journey to Heronden - about two miles away 'as the crow flies' (cross country). It was my job to drive these 25 sheep home alone. My route was westerly down Chennel Park Road, left into Cranbrook Road, joining the A28 to West Cross, Tenterden, turning right into Smallhythe Road, between the William Caxton Pub and Heronden Lodge Gate before turning right after a ¼ mile into the lane through Morghew Estate and on to Heronden.

Sheep not only suffer from maggot attacks, they are susceptible to a variety of ailments and diseases as are most farm livestock. Most common is worm infestation.

Animals needed to be drenched, an oral liquid treatment, originally a bottle was used for this purpose, later a gun-type syringe was introduced.

Use of both utensils required the animal to be caught and held while the exact dose was administered. Hard, dirty work.

Nowadays a 'pour-on' remedy can be used. Although sheep and cattle need to be penned fairly tightly for the application of the liquid, it is a much easier operation than the old 'catch and hold' way. Personal harm risk is reduced. You are less likely to have feet trodden on or limbs damaged with contact between animal and pen structure.

The treatment works similar to the 'Spot On' used for our domestic animals. The remedy penetrates the skin and enters the bloodstream when applied to the backs of sheep and cattle.

At one time we had a wayward bullock that needed catching for treatment, but all efforts to get the animal into a pen or building failed. No way was it going to be captured. My husband would not be beaten by some unruly creature. The only way, he reckoned, was to lasso it and anchor it to a gate post. Choosing a strong flexible rope and coiling it lariat fashion, he waited until the bullock was grazing steadily. Bob cast the rope, and as luck would have it, it fell neatly over its poll. In startled surprise, up came the bullock's head and the noose dropped under the jaw placing the rope firmly around the bullock's neck. That was the easy bit. Now to anchor it. This beast had other ideas. With a snort, it set off in desperation to rid itself of this encumbrance. Bob still had hold of the rope determined not to let go. An animal on four legs can run much faster than a man on two. The pair had not travelled far before Bob's legs couldn't keep up with the pace. He was unceremoniously pulled flat on his face. Still, he did

*Driving sheep from Potts Farm to
Heronden in 1961.*

not let go of the rope. He was
towed wild west rodeo-style
across the field through the
cowpats and a patch of stinging
nettles on some rough terrain
which turned him on his back,
yanking the rope from his
hands. The bullock had escaped
yet again.

The most devastating disease
is Foot and Mouth disease.
This highly contagious disease

spreads like wildfire amongst all cloven-footed animals.
Humans and non-cloven animals do not contract Foot and
Mouth disease, but all can be carriers.

Once a case of Foot and Mouth is confirmed, usually by a
Ministry vet, the entire herd and/or flock are destroyed and
their carcasses burnt.

Livestock movement is banned or restricted. No markets or sales are allowed.

During the last outbreak of the disease, I had booked seats at the Leas Cliff Hall in Folkestone to see Jethro, the Cornish comedian and was due to travel with my sister Christine and her husband Ivan. We decided not to go for fear of bringing the dreaded disease back with us. Folkestone being a port with much traffic and the disease is transportable on vehicle tyres.

On the evening of the show, on answering the telephone I was very surprised to hear a cheery voice saying "Hello, its Jethro here. The theatre tells me some of you farmers are not coming because of Foot and Mouth". There followed an amusing conversation which cheered us all up.

*Like father, like daughter. Julie in pursuit of a Charolais x calf.*

*Top right: Joan, Jack Pearce and Les Ramsden shearing.*

*> Les Ramsden from Appledore winding wool. He went on to win the Golden Shears award for Champion Sheep shearer in New Zealand.*

# Cattle

Over the years, cattle, both dairy and beef, have had to change to meet better productivity and the demands and requirements of consumers.

The lesser change has been among dairy breeds. Herds of red and white Ayrshires, the black and white British Friesian, the Channel Island breeds of the black-nosed Jerseys and the Golden Guernsey – remember Gold Top milk? – were common. The dual-purpose strawberry roan Shorthorn was often seen, also the Holstein Friesian, bigger and longer in the leg than the British Friesian. Both types of Friesian produced good beef calves, but the Holstein calves take 2-2½ years to mature.

The Native beef breeds – the compact black Aberdeen Angus, dark red Sussex, white-faced red Herefords and sandy Devon's. The Aberdeen Angus could be flighty (slightly wild, nervous, easily spooked), while the Sussex, Herefords and Devon's are more docile and easier to handle.

Beef bulls are used on the dairy breeds. For instance, Sussex x Fresians, the calves are usually black. Hereford x Fresian, the calves have black bodies and white faces.

Gradually, continental beef breeds arrived in this country. Belgium Blue, Charolais, Simmental and Limousin. Most of these bulls are massive, weighing over a ton. Crossed with our Native breeds they produce an excellent butcher's animal. With A.I. being readily available, it meant all farmers could choose the most suitable bull.

As teenagers, Bob and I were taught by our parents how to recognise a good young calf. It must be sturdy, with a strong head and a square backside. Not 'pin arsed!' Also, we learned how to bid at auctions. How to catch the auctioneer's eye, with a nod or wink or hand gesture, nothing too obvious, so as to alert any other person bidding.

In the mid-1960s, Bob and I took on the job of buying calves when required. Mostly at Ashford Market, sometimes Maidstone.

If calves were in short supply or of inferior quality, then we visited Heathfield Market. This was only a small market but at times we were able to buy a good calf at a reasonable price. Haywards Heath market was on the same day. Often more calves were purchased there to make up the load.

Father-in-law, Bob Luck Snr. had a farmer/cider maker friend, Sam Inch, who lived in Winkleigh, North Devon. Calves of better quality could be found there. It was decided it was worth a trip to Hatherly Market, near Okehampton in Devon.

Leaving Goodshill in the early hours on a Monday morning with our two girls asleep in the back of the van, we set off, arriving safely at Sam Inch's farm and there we were given refreshments. Next, we needed to find a B & B that also provided an evening meal.

Next morning, after breakfast, we drove for our first experience of Hatherly Market. It was busy and bustling. A good selection of calves, mainly Friesian and Hereford and Friesian crosses. Just what we were looking for. A close examination of the calves determined which ones we should bid for and set the top price we thought each calf was worth. We hoped to buy 10-12 calves. Mission completed, we returned to Sam Inch's, off-loaded the calves and fed them glucose and water. The calves were fed again next morning and then driven back home. There were more similar successful trips over several years.

# The Cider Maker's Wife

*< Calves at Heronden in the 1950s.*

*> A selection of calves at Hatherley Market about 1965.*

*At the Sheep Fair in Tenterden on the Recreation Field early 1960s.*

117

The two glucose feeds emptied the calves stomach of the original milk. The calf is less likely to scour on the change of milk.

Tenterden, Biddenden, Benenden and Sandhurst held sheep and cattle fairs – auction sales. Tenterden had a large May Fair that filled the Recreation Ground with pens of sheep and cattle. Animals were mainly moved to and from the sales on foot. The Recreation Ground was much bigger than it is today. There was no children's play area, toilets, tennis courts or car park on it. (See photo page 117).

Biddenden was the home of a two-day sale in early November. The first day saw the sale of sheep with cattle on the second day. Benenden and Sandhurst were single day sales on fields near the village centres. These sales brought the farming community together and business for locals shops and of the course, the pubs.

While farming at Crit Hall, Benenden, father-in-law entered twelve Charolais x yearling steers to be sold at Benenden Fair. I was entrusted to look after them at the sale with the instructions, "Don't give them away and don't bring them home!" The trade was not very brisk that day, bidding was slow. I had to do something quick. Picking out who was bidding, I started to bid myself, 'running up' the other bidders. When the price of the steers reached a decent level and I could see that there was only one other person interested and he was thinking hard about going higher. It was time to back out. I did not dare take them home. The hammer fell to the other farmer and all was well.

# Driving Cattle to Camber

In the mid to late forties, summer cattle keep (grazing) was acquired on land surrounding Camber Castle which is near Rye. The only way to get the animals there was to drive them by road. With a herd of cattle, this needed about five people, three ahead of the cattle, one would keep them steady preventing a stampede, one person either side of the road closing gates and preventing their entrance to any side roads or drives, and two people at the rear to stop any turning back. This rarely happens once the animals are on an open road they will keep going. Also, one of the rear guards could be called forward if necessary.

The journey was completed successfully without too many complications. The animals soon settled in their new surroundings and it was time to leave them and return home.

*Shorthorn x Sussex late 1940s/early 50s.*

Grandfather had driven his car behind them with me as the passenger. I had noticed some wallflowers growing from the castle wall fairly high up. I was unable to reach the blooms. I was hoisted up shoulder-high so that I was able to pick a few flowers to take back to my mother.

To the best of my memory, the drovers were Dickie Roberts, his two sons Charlie and Peter, my father, Leo Bignell and another farmhand whose surname was Penfold, but we always called him Penny.

*Julie with our Freisian herd about 1966.*

# Chickens

No farm was ever without chickens and in the days before battery and deep litter environments, could be afforded by most, free range was the natural culture; indeed, you found farmyards with birds domesticated by nature, but widely free most of the time, often laying away in the barn's haylofts and other buildings.

It was not an uncommon practice to occasionally take out a spade to turn over the ground for the hens. My mother Gladys often did this too, choosing to dig over the 'ammet casts' (Kent dialect for an ant hill) for them to feast on the eggs and ants themselves.

Of course, the hens were not respecters of danger and got in quickly as the spade turned over a new divot. I remember clearly an incident of the very unlucky mistiming of one eager pullet that ducked in for the bounty as the spade fell, severing its head at a stroke.

The loss of a pullet would be very annoying to my mother as often amongst farmers looking after poultry was a woman's responsibility. The eggs were after all not just for home consumption but for sale. They were collected daily and boxed for collection, the boxes themselves being left at the end of the farm road for Stonegate egg packers in Sussex.

As the birds were free range and running with a few cockerels some of the eggs would by the very nature of things be fertile.

Although the normal small, medium and large categories were the same as today, the price the family got for their eggs

121

depended on a few other criteria and price deductions were made for blood spots, meat spots, watery whites and hair cracks, not to mention incubator 'clears'.

The 'clears', so-called, were those initially intended for hatching but after a few days' incubation had been found to be infertile. The eggs would have been 'candled' using a very intense white light which showed up any small veins. The absence of any small veins would signify infertility. They were then most probably passed on for processing for such things as egg powder or even animal feeds.

# Children at work

As a youngster, I was always about the farm lending a hand, or so I thought, for at a very young age there were things I could not do, nor be allowed to attempt.

I was however never discouraged and wanted to help with the pea crop in the way the menfolk did, for mechanisation had reached the farm.

My first real job on the farm was in the summer holidays of 1947. I was then eight years old and the tractor purchased earlier now had a mower on it with a pea-lifting attachment. The peas were left to harvest until the haulm and pods turned brown and the peas were like little hard bullets (haulm is to peas as straw is to wheat). The mower would cut the peas, but when the tractor came round next time, if the peas had not been moved, then the wheels would run over the already-cut peas and crush them. A gang of farm hands around the field would move the peas away with pitchforks so that the tractor didn't run over them when it came around next time.

I was begging my parents to be allowed to do this job and they said yes, I could, but I wasn't old enough to use a pitchfork to do the work. Instead, I was given a strod stick – a stick cut from a hazel tot – the wooden equivalent of a pitchfork, so I could play my part in the pea harvest. Hazel was used for its durability and suppleness. It absolutely lasts forever. (See picture page 47).

Another task I helped with was gathering up dock roots. These prolific tuberous weeds were very difficult to eradicate. After a field had been ploughed, cultivated, seeded and harrowed, the dock roots would come up to the surface.

A group of people using all sorts of receptacles, buckets, sacks, trugs, anything that would hold these dock roots, would set to work across the fields, picking up these roots. When gathered up they were laid up on top of the hedge so that they couldn't grow again – or hopefully. But I know, after a period of up to 12 months, if a dock root falls down from the hedge, it will grow again.

Insecticides and weed killers were not yet in everyday use in those days and just as wild oats were picked out by hand from the standing crops, so at the ploughing stage, weeding was done by hand too.

I had a friend who had one of these strange roots given her as an exotic plant and to her disgust, after several weeks of nurturing, discovered it to be just another 'bloody' dock.

The only good thing about docks is that the sap from crushed dock leaves neutralises the acid from stinging nettles.

# Fruit

Of course, apples and cherries figured very highly as a fruit crop in those days, but there have been major changes in the shapes and height of fruit trees since the 1940s.

There are still today orchards of old trees, shaped and pruned horizontally and not exceeding 12ft or so: the newer orchards are bred to grow no more than 6-7ft and are planted much closer together. This is the progress towards ease of picking, sometimes by machine.

It is rare nowadays to find the trees that were common then – cherry trees 25ft tall and apple and pear trees nearly as high.

Enter then the long-forgotten apple ladder which was a massive construction, some 26ft or so high, very broad-based perhaps three foot across and tapering to a very narrow, sometimes pointed top.

These ladders were pushed through the branches from the bottom, up through the tree, whereafter the fruit picker armed with a sack-bag ascended, to pick the fruit without bruising it.

Anyone with vertigo would have had instant punishment, for these ladders weren't far removed from the big top, such was the precarious nature of the occupation.

On one particular day, it transpired that my ever-willing presence was required by the others to climb the ladder and pick the top fruit on the lighter branches, in the knowledge that my lighter weight on the ladder would be of benefit. But, when it was suggested that having picked all I could reach, the ladder was to be erected on the slippery steel flatbed of the lorry, the overall situation began to look decidedly dangerous. Seeing this danger I baulked at the opportunity, running off and calling back, "If you want those apples picked that way, you can pick 'em yourselves!"

The farm had a large number of cherished cherry trees with deep red, sweet fruit.

There was one rather annoying problem for my grandfather, Tom Clarke, and that was the somewhat large population of rooks that bred in plague proportions in the nearby woods.

Nature, it seems, conspires to produce cherries to coincide with the rearing of rook chicks and as no such things as automatic or gas-driven bird scarers existed, Grandfather's ingenuity was put to the test to preserve his crop.

Grandfather knew that just as a flock of geese can clear a field of pasture in a day, so a flock of hungry rooks could pick the best of his fruit in a few hours.

Now everyone knows that farmers get up early, if it's not for the milking, then it'll be to attend to the stock in some form or another. But, the maddening thing is that those shiny black feathered corvids could always get up earlier.

Determined not to lose his valuable crop, he devised a bird scarer of primitive, if not intricate design, somewhat reminiscent of 'Heath Robinson' proportions.

The design consisted of two large sheets of corrugated iron placed and suspended in such a way that a further two pieces of old iron could be made to swing into them at the pull on a long piece of binder twine. The twine ran through the branches over and under the fence wire and thence to and through his bedroom window.

To effectively work this contraption a certain degree of effort was required, as the friction on the route of the twine, coupled with the weight of the iron conspired to make the need for a good old 'yank'.

A trial proved, with a certain amount of pride, that the noise generated by the irons banging the corrugated sheets simultaneously would do the business. Such was his pride

*Another way of birdscaring – Cherry pickers, Dickie Bacon with shotgun and Mary Bacon holding the child.*

that he demonstrated his device to Dad, his son-in-law, and blossomed in his approval.

Grandfather's bedroom overlooked the cherry orchard, from where he could survey the masterpiece he had designed and he went to bed feeling that once the fruit was ripe, he at least was ready for the feathered invaders.

The harvest did indeed blossom, and subsequently ripen, and true to his convictions, the hungry black gang of thieves arrived. Fortunately, the rooks can't do things as quietly as they should and Grandfather was ready for them. Still clad in his long johns he sat on the edge of his bed and yanked the twine. The flock rose in a cacophony of sound and fled.

The problem was, it was still only dawn, not long past 4am, so Tom got used to sleeping with the twine tied to his wrist so as to save him getting out of bed and enabling him to steal a further hour of sleep.

Now it so happened that Dad was up very early one morning to see to a sick calf and on the way past the cherry orchard he could see the cloud of rooks gathering.

Having been given a demonstration on the workings of the patent device he was anxious to give it another go, so he nipped into the orchard, grabbed hold of the twine, and remembering the instructions, gave the twine an almighty yank.

Now Grandfather was certainly not awake until that is, he was pulled unceremoniously from his bed by the twine wrapped firmly around his wrist.

Crows were always a problem to arable and fruit farmers, as well as the finches that took off all the buds just before the spring broke. Grandfather would have needed a very long piece of twine to protect his acreage from the black devils. One way he devised, in the face of much scepticism from his peers, was the use of painted anthracite. This fuel you will recall came in ragged lumps, black and grey, the colour of rooks' plumage. Grandfather splashed selected lumps with red paint and scattered them strategically over the field and swore blind it was effective. Of course, the sceptics among his friends argued crows were carrion eaters anyway and this method would attract them, not scare them off. Even Aesop knew crows were clever, remembering the stones in the pot fable, but Grandfather was undeterred and continued to have faith in the practice.

Perhaps though, the belt and braces approach may have been a slight admission of doubt, because he did build a most realistic scarecrow in his endeavours to protect his seeds.

Indeed, as though to prove the authenticity there was the incident with the old dog Meg who came into the yard barking and whining in such a state as to alarm the household.

Each time Grandfather approached Meg, the dog backed off away, circling and barking some more. It didn't take long for the penny to drop either, for he could see the dog wanted him to follow, and follow he did – out of the farmyard, through the gate and right up to the bloody scarecrow!

# Threshing and other Winter Tasks

The hedges were cut annually, usually in October, using what was known locally as a bagging hook, which is better known as a sickle and a hook stick, which was an improvised hand rake cut from a piece of hazel with a handle about 18 inches to 2 feet long, with a hook on the end. The wooden hook assisted in pulling the grass to one side on the banks of ditches to make it easier for cutting. The grass cut was used for litter in the cattle yards.

Traditionally coppicing of woodland always took place between October and February, while the sap is down (the tree is resting). Chestnut is cut every 12 to 20 years. The younger growth is suitable for spiles (fencing stakes), fencing and gate making and some smaller hop poles. The 20-year growth is required in the hop gardens and must be at least 18 feet long where extra support is paramount, on corners and the perimeter.

The tool for the job was a woodcutter's felling axe, long before chainsaws existed. Chestnut grows tall and straight with few branches on its trunk. The top (canopy) is removed and set aside ready to be made into faggots.

Where the woodland is mixed, other trees such as Ash and Hornbeam are cut to provide fuel for next year for use in open fires. Chestnut spits (throws out sparks) and is therefore dangerous for indoor use on open fires.

The thresher always brought an air of excitement. The golden summer harvest is on its last journey. The tractor positions the machine alongside the stacks, their thatched roof already removed. Wire netting is placed around the stack to catch the rats as they leave the 'sinking ship'. The long, wide belts are attached to the thresher and the pulley on the side of the tractor engine. One man climbs a ladder to reach the stack top, another onto the thresher. The tractor starts, the belts whine, the first sheaf is dropped to the man (feeder) on the machine. Everything is in motion. In goes the first sheaf, followed by a steady continuation. The screeds within the thresher move and vibrate until the grain is separated from the straw. Large thick hessian sacks are secured to catch the flow of corn. When filled and tied, the sacks will hold 2¼ cwt. The threshed straw comes out loose at the back and is tied into bundles called a 'truss'. Later years saw a baler positioned to take the straw straight in. (See photos pages 53-57).

The 'caving', outer husk of the grain was deposited on the ground underneath the thresher. One might think there would be little use for this material, but in wartime and after in the era of 'make do and mend', this fairly soft, but durable commodity had a variety of uses. After being oven-dried, the caving could be used for stuffing pillows and cushions. Even making a mattress for babies cots. I remember helping my mother to scoop up 'cavings' into an old pillowcase when Joan and David were expected.

The highest grade of wheat grain went for milling for flour and bread making. The smaller grain was used for animal and poultry feed. I remember taking grain to Ashbourne Mill, the water mill near Rolvenden Station where it could be rolled, crushed or ground. Standing on the back of the lorry, I could peer through the mill doorway and see the large white paddles turning as they entered the fast-flowing water that had journeyed down from the Mill Pond itself (I previously lived at Mill Pond Farm). The paddles, in turn, operated the cogs that turned the heavy stones that made the flour.

All seemed covered in white dust, including Miss Dorothy Millen the mill owner, who lived with her mother in the adjoining house. Assistant, Harry Reed, was a relative of Dandy Field Snr. and son Wilf who had a grocery shop near the War Memorial. At the end of the day, Harry would be seen cycling home looking like a ghost.

*Threshing with steam engine. Note the round cornstack.*

# Bob and I

When Bob and I got back together on his 30th birthday 1960, after splitting up for nearly a year, we both knew that it was for life.

A trip to the Hastings and Bexhill areas delivering cider in the old long wheelbase grey farm Land Rover, piled high with 4½, 6 and 10-gallon wooden barrels and the two gallon stone jars with Bob Luck Ltd, Cider Makers, Benenden etched on them does not sound very romantic.

It was a warm August evening and I was able to discard my working clothes of t-shirt and jeans and wear a pretty dress and sandals.

Customers were both commercial and private, some being farms who purchased the not-so-strong cider to quench the thirsty workers at harvest. When the Hastings deliveries were completed, we bought fish for our families at the fish market in the Old Town. A good-sized Plaice was 6d (2½p) and Turbot was 2/6d per lb. (12½p). Then we set off for Bexhill driving along the seafront past Hastings Pier. Ships were visible in the channel on this clear evening. We didn't chat the whole journey. We had known each other a long time. We were at ease and comfortable knowing one another's thoughts.

Both of us had grown up on, and were working on our family's farms. Our interests were similar. The countryside, wildlife, horse racing, hunting and fishing. Bob did not ride and I didn't like sea fishing. I am no sailor. There were no problems with this.

*Our wedding day, July 14th 1962 at Ashford Registry Office.*

*With Bob's brother Michael, Bob Snr, baby Ann and grandfather Tom Clarke.*

*Mackerel fishing in the summer of 1962 with Geoff Pay and Jim Jennings.*

*Mum and Dad 1970.*

*Goodshill Farmhouse on the Cranbrook Road, Tenterden.*

*With Ann and Julie at Goodshill.*

*Julie and Ann in late 1960s.*

*Julie and Ann in 1965 on a Sussex x cow.*

*Julie and Ann with a black calf at Benenden, late 1960s.*

We were not desperate to get married. We saw each other most days of the week, either at work or socially and generally enjoyed our lives and company.

In the Spring of 1962, I discovered that I was pregnant. We had to tell our parents, so we decided on a Sunday night that we'd both do it, the next day, on a Monday morning. I was doing the washing with Mum and the opportunity arose for me to tell her of my suspected pregnancy.

"What did you go and do that for?" She was angry.

Grandfather came in. "What's up?"

"Well, she's gone and got herself in the family way."

And he said, "Well, so did you, didn't you?" She didn't have an answer to that.

Bob and I got engaged and then married on Bastille Day, July 14th.1962 at Ashford Register Office at 9.30am in the morning. The reception was held at the Vine in Tenterden. We spent a week on honeymoon in Looe, Cornwall. While there, Bob managed to go sea fishing and caught a shark.

Ann was born on 7th January 1963.

Like today's young people we couldn't afford to buy a house. Bob and I spent 2½ years living in 2-3 rooms with his parents in Goodshill House. We had a bedroom and a sitting room, containing a little cooker. The bedroom had a washbasin just inside the door with a mirror over it. At twenty to six each morning, father-in-law would come in, put the light on and tell Bob to get up, and go out and get the cows in, while he went off to Benenden to collect the post in case there were any cider orders for that day. There was no privacy.

Ann and Julie were born at Goodshill House Farm.

Father-in-law had a pair of cottages built on part of the orchard in 1965. Bob, Ann, Julie and I were to have a brand new home. Our wedding presents, consisting of all types of household requisites were no longer redundant. Most of the furniture we bought at a local auction sale room. My sisters, Joan and Christine, helped make curtains and other soft furnishings.

Bob was no house husband. He did not believe in helping to wash up. That was a 'woman's work'. If there were no clean cups or glasses, he'd use a dirty one. His cooking skills were non-existent but to my knowledge, he did have two attempts. The first just before we married. Feeling hungry after a late night out, he scanned his mother's well-stocked larder and decided on a tin of pasta (Ravioli) in tomato sauce. The cooking instructions on the tin were "Place in boiling water and heat for 10 mins". Bob found the saucepan, popped in the can and filled with water to halfway up the can as instructed. Feeling quite pleased with himself he settled down with his dogs on their old camp bed. Two things went wrong – first he'd forgotten to puncture the can, secondly, he fell asleep. He got a rude awakening when the pot boiled dry and the can exploded, shooting the contents skywards hitting the ceiling, the majority of which fell down onto the kitchen table, covering his mother's pile of neatly laundered clothes in sticky tomato sauce. Bob hastily turned off the electric, binned the ruined pot and can and crept up to bed, still hungry.

On a later occasion, Bob had a go at frying eggs. Pan on the stove with a little oil. Now to add the eggs, but he didn't realise they had to be cracked over the pan, not by the fridge. After six eggs had ended up on the floor, much to his frustration, but to the delight of the terriers, that meal was abandoned.

Sometime later, Bob was off shooting with two of his mates, one had recently purchased a brand new washing machine. Bob was invited in, by the proud owners, to see it working.

Bob somewhat bemused by all the fuss and ado over a mechanical object, when asked for his opinion, muttered,

"Um, well, yeah. I married one of them".

In the Spring of 1967, father-in-law sold the 200 acres at Heronden that he had bought from my grandfather in 1959 to John Leroy of Leroy Tours who had recently bought the Morghew estate. Bob and I were both very sad at this. Bob loved the place as much as I.

Goodshill House Farm was a mere 97 acres and was insufficient to support the whole family. It was sold and the 240-acre Crit Hall Farm at Benenden was purchased. Crit Hall had in the past been owned by Lord Vesty who bred beef bulls there for export to Argentina.

There were four cottages at Crit Hall. Bob and I were allotted South Cottage in Nineveh Lane, which stood on its own. Brick built with two bedrooms.

It was while we were living there that I bought the girls their first pony, a black Shetland cross named Bonny. I taught them to ride. The pony could be naughty, bucking them off when he thought he had done enough. I stopped him doing this with a couple of stripes across his backside. He never bucked again, instead, he would lie down.

To help afford the pony and attending shows, I reared New Zealand White rabbits and calves.

One pair of rabbits soon produced plenty more. The calves bought in Ashford Market at about one week old were brought up on the bucket (milk supplement). Weaned at six weeks when they ate hay and calf nuts (crushed corn with added minerals and vitamins).

Animals reared this way are quiet and tame, easy to handle and will follow you. The kids often played with them and sat on their backs, especially the last two, a Black Sussex x Friesian heifer and a black and white Friesian steer.

In 1969 the drink driving law was passed. It wasn't long before Bob was stopped by Police and breathalysed. He was over the limit. He lost his driving licence for 12 months.

For transport he reverted to riding an old bicycle he had cadged off someone.

After a short time Bob said it was hard work and that in a year's time, he said: "I will either be like Charles Atlas (Body Builder) or dead".

It didn't come to either, because shortly after he was on his way home on a dark night down our narrow lane, when as Bob put it "I ran out of road", ended up upside down in the ditch underneath the buckled bike, with the only light broken and missing somewhere in the thorn hedge.

*Ann and Julie selling strawberries by the house at Crit Hall with Bob Luck Snr and Frank Relf,*

*'Porky & Bess' at Wealden Heights*

Faced with the situation of no motor transport, I didn't drive at that time. Shopping and getting the children to school was difficult. In 1970 father-in-law bought Wealden Heights, opposite Crit Hall. After some redecorating and a new Rayburn cooker being installed, we moved in.

This property had about four acres with it and a couple of outbuildings. Ideal for the ponies a few calves and some pink squealing weaner pigs.

Bob and I had lived in close proximity with his family for nearly ten years, which brought all circumstances in this sort of relationship, under everyone's feet, getting on each other's nerves, at times causing arguments and upset.

We longed to have a place of our own, a small farm that we could work together while we were still relatively young.

Bob's parents knew this and in the Autumn of 1972, we looked at two likely properties. The second was Mill Pond Farm, St. Michael's, situated at the end of a half mile private concrete drive. Remote but not isolated as it was previously part of the adjoining farm. We fell in love with it. It was a grass farm and some woodland extending to sixty-two undulating acres. A nice range of buildings, suitable for a variety of uses. The dwelling was a two-bed Colt bungalow. Cooking and water heating by way of a solid fuel AGA. Heating by solid fuel stove.

There was just one drawback, there was not any electricity. The lighting was by Calor Gas. I had grown up without electricity. To me, this was not a problem. It was connected in the summer of 1975. The property was for sale By Tender. The closing date mid-December. On the day in question, Bob had the day off to go sea fishing. On learning that the bid had been successful, I rang the boat owner's family, to convey the news to Bob, who managed to contact the boat at sea. Bob was so surprised and pleased, he almost fell overboard.

On January 24th, 1973, a wet miserable day, using the old Nuffield 10/60 tractor and a trailer we left Wealden Heights, Benenden for Mill Pond Farm, St. Michael's.

Apart from our household stuff we had very little in the farming line. The only livestock was one pig and one calf.

About the time of our move, we had been offered the pig swill (leftover food) from Benenden School, where Princess Anne was educated. Asking around we soon found other available sources. We invested in a large steam boiler and tank to cook the swill. This was required by law through MAFF, now DEFRA. A building also had to be converted because the raw and cooked swill must be kept separate to avoid any contamination.

Two in-pig sows were purchased and some weaners. A neighbouring friend brought his sheep in to graze the land during the winter months. This brought in a little income while the weaners were growing. When they reached the weight of five scores (100 lbs), they were sold as porkers.

We could only afford one vehicle. A van was necessary for all the various uses on the farm plus social work.

The 5cwt Ford we had was too small. A Leyland Sherpa was purchased. Boards were installed behind the seats and along the sides to prevent damage from the swill bins which were metal, dustbin-like containers.

One day travelling out from the farm to collect the girls from school, still carrying full bins of raw swill, I was approaching a sharp corner on the narrow concrete road, suddenly I was face to face with an oncoming car. The force of the emergency stop, brought the loose swill bins sliding at an increasing speed until they hit the board behind my seat. The impact of bin against board, sent the contents upwards, hitting the van roof, then descending, covering me with baked beans, custard and gravy!

Gradually we increased the pigs to a capacity of 150. Swill had to be collected and cooked most days. As well as feeding and watering, the pigs required cleaning out about twice a week.

One year it came to pass that the pigs would need cleaning out on Christmas Day or at a stretch, Boxing Day. Neither of us fancied this task on either day. We never had a holiday, but a few hours relaxation wouldn't come amiss.

It was decided that we would do the mucking out on Christmas Eve and with some extra clean straw bedding the pigs would be quite comfy for three days.

Christmas Eve dawned frosty white and crisp with a glimmer of the sun, about 8 am. Using two wheelbarrows we began the work. I loaded one barrow with fork and shovel, then Bob wheeled it around the buildings to the now quite large dung maxen which had been built up so that it now resembled a ski slope. A piece of weldmesh measuring 6'x3'x2" mesh was laid on the slope for easy access for the barrow to be pushed to the apex and tipped out. I had filled the second barrow but Bob had not returned with the empty.

Eventually, he came in, dumped the barrow and grimaced, holding his ribs.

"What's up", I asked. "Well", said Bob, "I took a run up the slope to gain momentum when my wellington's (wet from slurry) slipped on the weldmesh, legs spinning Andy Capp fashion, just as I tipped the barrow, I fell onto the upturned handles". He had broken his ribs.

To help fund the livestock we were cutting wood for pulp (paper making). All in all, it was hard, dirty work. We did not miss TV in the evening. All we wanted was some sleep. Our day started at 6 am.

One morning we both awoke with the flue. Couldn't get our heads off the pillow. It was unusual for us both to be ill at the same time, but we never did anything by halves.

*The Bingham Plucking Machine.*

*> With two 22lb geese and the
Bingham Plucking Machine 1986.*

*At the end of a heavy plucking day with Bob.*

*Hens at Mill Pond Farm.*

*Otto with Geese at Mill Pond.*

Our friend, Nigel Kemp came to help with the work until we were on our feet again. Realising we had too much to handle, we scaled down the pigs and bought some calves. Several died after contracting pneumonia.

The cost of the calves and vet bills, plus losing the animals made a hole in our resources. Diversification was needed or we would go bust.

Still keeping a few pigs, we branched out into poultry. 100 day-old meat chicks arrived at Ashford Railway station once a month for me to collect plus 50 Aylesbury ducklings at various intervals.

Ducks can be hand plucked successfully, but the chickens grow quickly and the skin is very tender, especially the pullets and would tear easily, if picked by hand, spoiling the appearance and overall presentation.

A secondhand Bingham Machine was the answer.

The Bingham Plucking Machine is a free-standing piece of equipment. Operated through belts via an electric motor at the base. The pulleys on which the belts run drives a spindle running through eight round plates. Spring screws adjust the tension. The more it rattles, the better it picks. The rotating plates suck in the feathers when the bird is held close to the machine. The bird must be manipulated and turned, keeping the skin fairly tight to prevent tearing or worse.

The wing and tail feathers have to be removed before being applied to the machine. These feathers are too stiff for the picker to cope with.

My plucking method was as follows... starting at the tail, along the back to the neck, supporting the body, the legs are next, one by one and then the wings. This way opened up the feathers to deal with the delicate breast.

Some tidying was necessary in the presence of short or broken plumage and/or stubs (new feathers just coming through the skin).

The feathers were expelled at the rear of the machine into a large sack. The body feathers of ducks and geese were valuable in good, clean condition. Chicken feathers were of little value and usually ended up in the dung maxen to eventually be used as fertiliser.

More income was needed. We both went out to work part-time. I went to work in the hops from stringing in February, dressing in March and training from April to June. Thereafter strawberry picking. Working on the hop picking machine in September. Bob went to work for an agricultural contractor haymaking and straw baling and carting. Also loading bines at hop picking.

In addition to farming Mill Pond, Bob and I still helped out with the cider making at Frogs Hole each year from September to the end of November. This ended in 1978 when Old Bob died.

The contract with Taunton Cider Co. had been relinquished, meaning the apples required for producing 100,000 gallons of juice for them were no longer needed. Plenty of pressing took place to produce the cider for the company, Bob Luck Cider Ltd, for subsequent years. The best/vintage cider matured after fermentation and sugaring, in 140-gallon barrels for 4 years. This strong, 22% proof drink was also known as the 'Apple Wine of Kent'.

# Cider Making

For the benefit of readers who have not read my previous book *'As Luck Would Have It'*, I will repeat a section here about Bob Luck Cider making.

...the whole family was to share a moment of distinction when on Sunday the 31st October 1971 an Independent Television Co. sought permission to transmit a programme called 'Farm Progress' It featured Bob Luck and Family from Frogshole Farm, Benenden in Kent and also John Bligh of Red House, Benenden, his main apple supplier.

Narrated by Mark Jenner, this is part of the transmission

*"...the Luck family at Benenden make 70,000 gallons of it* [cider] *a year, stored in barrels.*

*Mr Luck started in 1935, with a small hand press on an 18-acre farm. It was a bad first year, apples for cider making were in short supply and local farmers who customarily bought–in, or made, 30-120 gallons of cider couldn't restock. Mr Luck managed to acquire some apple juice at this time and that's how the business began.*

*His cider helped supplement the wartime beer ration and in 1945 he installed heavy plant and hydraulic presses.*

*In the press room apples of all varieties and type drawn from local growers are elevated up to a mill for pulping. As pulping continues the press is gradually built up in a series of wooden frames called mats – about fifteen in all.*

*The pulp won't be wasted. After pressing, it will be carted later to the fattening of cattle and sheep on Mr Luck's farm. The Luck's reckon you can fatten a bullock on apple pulp.*

*There's not much juice from pulping. What there is, flows with the rest into a holding pit for 300 gallons later to be pumped into barrels. When there are enough mats containing the pulp, they are moved across to the big 100 ton hydraulic presses that exert a pressure of half a ton per square inch and this is where the apple juice really flows.*

*There are two Luck brothers. The elder, Bob Luck junior, is in charge of the press room and his wife Evelyn works with him. They also tend and feed the stock.*

*The 120-gallon wooden casks are the main means of storing Bob Luck's cider, and the juice flowing from the presses is pumped straight to them via the holding pit.*

*From them, after further processing, will come ordinary cider, at 7-8% proof, and the apple wine of Kent better known as vintage cider, at 22-23% proof.*

*These are vintage cider barrels. White sugar is 'fed' to the cider to promote fermentation and it may stay in cask two to three years. It's pretty potent. The term 'vintage' in this case has nothing to do with the year or one particular harvest.*

*Out of cask, the cider must be purified by various methods and here Michael Luck, the younger brother, is in charge. He uses centrifuges to dissipate any solids in the cider – for example any specks of pulp which might have got through.*

*The cider is then passed through two separate filters. In one of them a special powder is introduced which coats the filter plates and improves filtration.*

*The liquid which finally goes into cask or jar, whether ordinary or vintage cider, will be bright and clear. It is sold in the cask, in gallon or half gallon jars and it costs 10 new pence a pint for ordinary and 12 new pence a Pony glass for vintage cider – the wine of Kent.*

*It is largely local retailing, through the pubs, off-licenses and cider bars, roughly travelling over a 30 mile radius from Frogshole Farm which includes the big coastal towns.'*

The transmission ended with the usual thanks to their hosts and the toast 'Here's Luck.'

*Bob Luck Senr. with cider jars in the bottling plant.*

*Bob Luck Cider jars.*

*Lorry tipping apples into pit.*

*Bessie the Collie watching apples going up on elevator.*

*Apples on the elevator.*

*Bob and George Parker with centrifuge filter for clearing impurities in the cider.*

*Cider jars and plastic barrels in the bottling plant.*

*Evelyn with cider barrels at Frogshole Farm, Benenden.*

*Evelyn pumping cider into barrels, 1970.*

No doubt old Bob thought the programme good for business or he would never have entertained it, he could, there was no doubt, have put more zing into the narrative with some of his catch phrases; *There's a baby in every bottle*, *Air raid tonic*, *Love potion* and many others. Of course, this pleasing twenty minute television programme with its warm sunny soft spoken narrator, its highly skilled camera crew panning around Frog's Hole belies the reality of Cider making. Like many country programmes, the 'down your way' balmy day image with its canned 'birds song, running stream, insect buzzing' sound tracks bear little resemblance to the rigours that often accompanied the work.

The Cider maker's day began at 7.30 am and finished at 5pm or was supposed to, but you can't stop in the middle of a process and you weren't finished until you'd cleaned up; making Cider is a messy business.

The apples came in all sorts of containers, not just in clean neat 40lb bushel boxes like in the film. They came in 'sacks' 'bulk bins', 'tipper trailers' and lorries, and were tipped at the foot of an elevator which carried them up into the mill. In the mill they were chopped up mechanically into pulp. Because of the acidity of the fruit all the metal coming into contact with it was stainless steel. The mill held 37 bushels of pulped apples [37x40lbs=1480 lbs (approx. 672 kilos)] measured auto-matically. Below the mill was a track supporting a stainless steel tray about 6" deep by 2'6" square. In the tray was laid a semi-rigid mat made of woven osier willow and on top of this was placed a wooden frame and over that laid diagonally was a square nylon sheet.

The pulp could be released to fall from the mill above in measured quantities. Two operatives standing either side of the frame would spread the pulp with their hands and then fold the corners of the nylon sheet into the middle before adding yet another tray. The act of folding the cloths in this way was called making 'a cheese'. This process was repeated until the progressive number of trays had reached the right height to fit under the press.

At this stage the operative's arms are cold, wet and sticky to the elbows.

The three hydraulic presses were electric made by H. Beare & Sons of Newton Abbot. Their capacity was one and a half tons to the square inch. All the presses had a linked drainage system of pipes to a 300-gallon underground collection chamber. Some varieties of apples were better than others, the worst being over-ripe Cox's and Worcesters because they were soft and not very juicy, their pulp was very slippery which made pressing slow and difficult.

If rushed, the cheeses didn't hold up and had to be rebuilt.

Although rubber boots and aprons were worn, when a bulge in one of the cheeses appeared there was little warning before, under such pressure, a huge jet of ice cold apple juice would drench the operator.

My hair had to be washed every evening and my trousers stood up on their own, amusing though it may seem it must be remembered that the apple juice wasn't warm and in the winter often only a degree or two above freezing.

The mill held 37 bushels of pulped apples, in theory measured precisely, however if the apples were larger than usual then the elevator fed them into the pulp mill faster than the pressings could be built up. So here we have a Charlie Chaplin *Modern Times* scenario where automation goes berserk.

'The elevator is lifting the fruit and the fruit is being pulped and delivered at such a rate that the operatives can't keep up.' Well not exactly. One burst cheese and the mill must be stopped by tripping the elevator circuit as the mill continues all the while it is being fed by the elevator. The operatives can tell if the mill is full by the sound of the knives in the mill, but if the mill was very full, stopping the elevator did not 'immediately' stop the mill delivering, especially if the apples were large, so the operatives continued to be supplied with sticky cold apple pulp dripping down on them from the overflowing mill.

Having drained all the juice the trays then had to have the pulp [sometimes referred to as mash or pomace] removed. This now has the appearance of cardboard both in colour and consistency and in some cases stubbornness as the Cox's left sticky lumps clinging to the cloths. The pulp was used as cattle feed and they seemed to fatten well on it. As Bob said at the time, the ITV film didn't show them skidding about in their wellies, soaked to the skin and frozen to the bone. It didn't show the wasps and the annoying legions of fruit flies or the back breaking loading and lifting that went with the production, it didn't even say that after all, such a fine product's reputation wasn't earned without hard work.

Outside the mill were rows of barrels bought in from such firms as Allan, Skinner & Parr of London and Ellis Son & Vidler of Hastings. They had been used before for Wine, Rum or even Whisky. The sizes varied 140, 120, 60 and 48 gallons being usual. They were filled under pressure not always without mishap as it was not unknown for the pressure to blow the head out of the barrel instead of coming back through the bung.

Fermentation of course begins after filling. To this day some producers rely on the natural sugars and yeasts on the actual apples to trigger fermentation for rough cider. In old Bob's case the quality was important to him and whereas he produced many varieties, his vintage cider, so-called, was consistently good, being between 22 and 23 percent proof after four years in the barrel. This product attracted the Customs & Excise officers regularly to take samples and to set the appropriate duty. It was not of course just the appeal of the alcohol content but the rich colour given it by the Demerara sugar and the mellow smoothness that categorised it as 'vintage' not in the sense of old wine but in the sense of fine quality.

Other less meritorious ciders were produced some even sweetened with saccharin, as the market demanded all grades. Two gallon stone jars complete with screw cap and tap and the words 'Bob Luck Cider' were the best sellers and are still seen today in antique shops around the south east. One gallon, glass demi-johns, one and two-litre bottles catered for all demands. Alas, the demise of the Bob Luck cider industry preceded the introduction of cans, currently the most efficient way of selling small amounts in large quantities, a system that would no doubt have appealed to old Bob's business sense.

Old Bob's business sense carried as always an air of humour. His lorries carried the greeting on the front 'Here's Luck' and on the tail board 'Cheerio!' initially, later versions added the words 'and Bob's your Uncle!'

We had always had a few geese. Their staple diet is grass. It is reckoned 3 geese will eat as much grass as one sheep daily and they would keep the grass under control in awkward places and their large white eggs could be sold during their spring laying season.

Goose was becoming popular as Christmas Dinner. Why not embrace this market? We contacted everyone possible in search of broody hens to hatch the goose eggs. Geese are not good mothers. A large hen (e.g. Rhode Island Red) will cover four goose eggs. I soon had broody hens sitting in every mode of accommodation, in any nook and cranny available. The incubation period is 28-30 days. Very rarely was every egg fertile. After four weeks the goslings hatched, yellowy green in colour, which denotes their adult colour, the lighter colour will be white, the darker, grey. The hen is very proud of her brood, fluffing up her feathers and pecking when approached. She teaches her babies to eat and drink, clucking, calling and indicating with her beak where food and water are, but does not appreciate it when the goslings take a bath and shake themselves, giving her a shower.

This method of hatching continued for about two years. The old breeds of egg layers were rapidly replaced by more economic hybrids who laid more eggs for less food but rarely became broody. An alternative had to be found for incubation. We found a place at East Peckham with a custom-built incubator. We would travel over every week taking eggs and bringing goslings home.

At the peak, we were rearing 350 geese, plus 200 chicken and 100 ducks for the Christmas market. Picking began early December to supply butchers, hotels and restaurants, also a lot of birds had to be 'dressed' for local people who needed the birds oven-ready. We also provided a game plucking service. I didn't care for this job. Many of the birds were badly shot with shattered bones. The sharp splintered pieces, sometimes invisible, coated in blood clotted feathers, pierced hands and fingers quite often, resulting in a minor infection, leaving hands sore for several days, making all work, domestic and otherwise, painful. The healing process was slow due to re-occurrence.

Although help was employed at Christmas time, the work-load was heavy and causing aggravation to the back injury I suffered as a teenager. I was advised by an osteopath to "pack some of it up before it packs you up".

About this time a friend had approached us with a view to keeping his two horses with us. I wasn't keen on the idea. Bob argued that he was a friend and that it was alternative income. Shortly after, the two horses arrived, a golden

Palomino named *Commanche* and his skewbald mate *Cherokee*.

This was the beginning of another side of the business which steadily increased as the poultry was scaled down to about 40 geese for Christmas but we still reared quite a lot of meat chicken.

I took in a variable assortment of ponies and horses over the next 20 plus years. From cute but awkward Shetlands, Bay, Black and Chesnut, stout little animals, much stronger than they look. Show ponies, more delicately built, strutting their stuff with flowing manes and tails, groomed until their coats were like a mirror. Family ponies fit for a young inexperienced child to ride but also suitable for older children and Mum as well. Then there were the thoroughbreds. Most had not made the grade as racehorses. In inexperienced hands, these animals are lethal because they still have the racing instinct. They can be docile one minute and have a brainstorm the next. The worst incident I had was when a chesnut mare threw her young teenage rider, luckily not on the public road, galloped up the drive, jumped an oncoming car, crashed through a hedge ripping itself to pieces. A vet took two hours to clean and stitch the wounds.

I forbade the family to use her again. When she recovered from her injuries, she was sent to the West Country to become a broodmare.

I had the pleasure of evicting three other horses that had caused damage to the stables, fences and my garden. Two individual horses actually attacked me. I could have been injured had it not been for some quick thinking. I always remember what my mother taught me at an early age, "Animals are unpredictable, they have minds of their own", she told me. "Also, you have to think, what is the animal thinking? Bloody amateurs!"

In the late 1970s, the pulpwood trade diminished, so we then resorted to supplying firewood (logs). This was even harder work as the wood needed to be handled much more, and therefore time-consuming too. Most customers required different log sizes and we were expected to stack it. Very rarely was there a decent accessible shed in which to store the wood. All sorts of improvised accommodation was used, from old rusty tin shacks to narrow lean to's, to coal bunker type facilities.

It was on a Monday morning in May when there was a van load of logs to be delivered in Benenden, close to Crit Hall. As we were in need of a couple of suckler calves, after delivering the logs, we set off to Maidstone Market to hopefully buy the calves.

After looking over the calves and picking out two Black Sussex x Friesians, we were viewing the rest of the livestock awaiting the start of the auction when we were approached by two uniformed Police Officers and told that we must return immediately to Crit Hall. The officers said that they did not know why. Thinking that something must be amiss with Bob's mother, we left at once. Elder daughter Ann worked in Staplehurst and I did contemplate stopping to see if she was OK but decided against it. On entering Crit Hall, Bob's mother was alright, but she and Bob's Aunt Vera (Relf) and his brother Michael were all ashen-faced.

Ann had been killed on the road riding her little motorbike on the way to work.

The tragic loss of Ann devastated the whole family. Julie's life stopped for a considerable period. Bob went on the booze for several days until two of his friends took him out for the day. We all dealt with our grief in different ways. I was kept sane by rearing newly-hatched goslings and young chickens, generally throwing myself into the day to day running of the farm and home, but in times of stress I eat and eat I did – comfort eating if you like. Mostly sweet things like chocolate, biscuits and cake.

The only words spoken after Ann's death that stick in my mind were that of the vicar at her funeral. He said that "We must think of Ann tending the horses in heaven." Although those words did not mean much at the time, they have been a source of comfort at times since. I can see her as she was at home, just loving all to do with her beloved horses. Helping out at Pony Club Camp and encouraging a younger person. She was a brilliant rider and was competing in Showjumping with the likes of Marion Mould. Marion *nee* Coates had an Olympic pony named '*Stroller*'. She later married Royal N.H. Jockey David Mould. I am sure Ann would have beaten Marion had she lived.

Julie meanwhile was working for Margaret Hooker, successfully competing at show jumping, cross country and eventing.

During the next 10 months after losing Ann, my weight rocketed by nearly 2½ stone (35lbs, approx. 16 kilos). Julie was going to be 18 years old in May. Bob and I decided on a big party for her, so I must pull myself together and get in shape. I vowed to lose a stone in a month, and I did. It just takes willpower.

In 1982, Bob was experiencing a lot of pain in his ankle, giving him gip (pronounced Jip) as he described it. Bob had injured his ankle as a young man out shooting in the early Autumn. He had jumped off a gate, landing on the ground, where, in the springtime cattle hooves had made large indentations in the soft earth (poaching). The large, deep, ridged holes had been baked hard and unforgiving by the summer sun. Grimacing with pain and unable to bear weight on his leg, two of his companions helped him to a vehicle and he was driven home. The doctor was called, who diagnosed a bad sprain. The ankle was strapped up and he was told to rest it for a couple of days.

Now another visit to the same doctor was needed. Bob was sent for an x-ray, which showed that the ankle had been broken in three places and was now riddled with arthritis. An operation was required – a Triple Arthrodesis. This fused the joint so only up and down movement was possible.

Bob recovered sufficiently to do some work and to ride a bike again. I was at work in the hops for Gerald Orpin when I was told I needed to go to find Bob who had had some sort of accident on his way cycling into Tenterden. A van had clipped the handlebars of his bike, unseating him and sent him somersaulting across the Ashford Road. His injuries included broken ribs and clavicle (collarbone). I have never before or since seen such bruising. Glorious technicolour from shoulder to his bad ankle.

Arthritis set in to his hip. The hip was replaced at Easter 1986, at the age of 55, at St Saviours Hospital in Hythe. The van driver was prosecuted for dangerous driving and Bob did receive compensation which paid for his operation.

Gone were the days of hard work, no heaving bales of hay and straw. No wood cutting or mucking out pigs. He could, however, help with the poultry. He even became domesticated enough to bring the washing in! He went ferreting with his mates, took the dogs for a run and managed to do some rabbit shooting for dog food, but I had to take the car around the farm to bring him and the rabbits home.

At hop picking time, he could stand in the trailers to load the bines as they were cut. Of course, his disability did not stop him going to the pub or day trips to France.

In January 1989 we were dealt another blow when through medical reasons, I lost my driving licence. Bob was banned from driving in 1980 for five years after being breathalised again. It was agreed between us at the time that he would not drive again.

Now neither of us could drive, it posed quite a predicament. Where do we go from here? It was a worrying time for a few months. We had a small overdraught at the bank. It was impossible to know if we could continue to keep the farm going. For two months we either used public transport, which meant a one-mile walk to the nearest bus route, or expensive taxis. Julie helped out as much as she could, but she was in full-time work.

Towards the end of March, I found just what I had been looking for, a driving pony. An 11.2 hand strawberry roan Welsh Mountain pony with flaxen mane and tail, only 4 years old and green (inexperienced). Two weeks passed before I had the courage to drive Toby to Tenterden. He was very intelligent and learned his job quickly, which was taking out the farm produce and bringing home chicken feed and the like, groceries and even a new vacuum cleaner. Toby became quite a celebrity around the town and local villages, being widely photographed, once by a coach load of American tourists visiting a garden in St Michaels.

In late July 1991, I regained my licence and purchased a brand new Austin Maestro. Having not been behind the wheel for 2½ years I had slightly lost my confidence. David Turner, who was manager of Warrens Coaches, and who had taught Bob to drive, accompanied me to Ashford where I drove around the town until I became confident again. David asked how I felt. I told him that my heart had come up into my mouth several times – meaning that I was nervous. "Oh well", he said, "As long as it's gone back down you are OK".

I did not part with Toby though. He had looked after me for 2½ years. Now I was going to look after him. We used to give trap rides at fetes etc. On one occasion we had the honour of carrying the Mayoress Felicity Edwards in procession along Tenterden High Street from West to East Cross, sandwiched between the town crier, Harry Hickmott and a marching brass band.

When driving around the lanes Toby would suddenly pull over onto the grass verge, he had heard an oncoming vehicle. On one occasion it was a bin lorry which filled the road. He was an amazing little pony. I had him for 21 years.

At the age of 25, sadly he was put down, due to laminitis and Cushing's disease, whilst munching fresh grass in his favourite paddock, and that's where he was buried.

With the aid of taking sheep and cattle in for keep, some liveries, the poultry and some casual work we were able to keep the business afloat.

There was more trouble in 1987 in the wake of the hurricane. The wind blew the roofs off the pig pens, sending the asbestos crashing through the roof of an adjacent building which killed several fattening meat chickens. It felled 40 oak trees in ten acres of woodland, flattened the garden fruit trees, cut off power and electricity for ten days and phone lines for three weeks. The half-mile concrete drive plus lanes were strewn with trees, cutting us off for two days.

During the 1980s I suffered two more bereavements, that of my brother David aged only 37 in 1983 and my father Leo in 1988. He was 73.

Looking back, the 1980s was the most catastrophic, tragic, traumatic decade of my entire life.

Life has to continue and the best must be made of a bad job. The next decade was better to start with. I had my driving licence back. The eight black and white cross-bred puppies were born, presenting another challenge. First their rearing, then later learning and teaching the two kept pups, Dot and Otto, obedience and ring craft, which led to showing and

*Driving Toby my Welsh Mountain pony in the exercise cart.*

*Giving Pony and Trap rides at St Michael's School.*

165

meeting new people and eventually becoming a Dog Show organiser and judge.

August 1990 saw Bob's 60th birthday for which I held a barbecue and a clay pigeon shoot. The site was high up on the bank at Mill Pond Farm, overlooking the 10-acres of woodland opposite. The various greens of Oak, Ash and Hornbeam stood out. Two large Scots Pine pinnacle above all others. Lower down, where once long ago was part of the Mill Pond itself, Silver Willow and tall Alders are visible growing along the little river bank. Deep in the valley lies the lake, shimmering in the sun with some large carp popping in and out of the water. The top of the bank was fairly flat, making an ideal platform for the clay traps. Guns could choose their positions depending on whether they preferred low, medium or high birds.

I prepared the food and did the barbecue cooking. They all seemed to have an enjoyable time and it became an annual event, attracting around 40 friends and family.

*Bob's 60th birthday at Mill Pond Farm with Brian Martin, John Hook, Dave Moore, Peter Johns and others.*

# Julie's Wedding

While working for Tony Orlikowski, the Animal Feed Merchant from Bethersden, Julie had met Robert Wade. Robert became a regular visitor to the farm. The four of us enjoyed a few trips out horse racing as far afield as Huntingdon and Fakenham. A friend of Robert's owned a horse called *Hard Times* and indeed it was because it never made it to the winner's enclosure!

Even so, it was good to see another part of the country – the flat fenland in comparison to the undulating local Kent countryside – and to enjoy the hustle and bustle of such a meeting. Watching jockeys in colourful silks controlling fit, muscle-toned horses. Galloping and jumping at break-neck speed. The thrill of the chase, and tearing up betting tickets when our chosen animal failed to get into the first three. The joy when one horse romped home at 5-1, ensuring that we didn't come home on a 'flat tyre' (deflated).

About three years after they met, Julie and Robert announced their engagement.

The wedding was set for December 2nd, 1994. Like our wedding, it was to be at Ashford Registry Office.

Awaking early that morning we were greeted by thick fog – a real pea-souper. Nevertheless, we arrived in Ashford safe and sound. Parking in the old Ashford Market, we walked across Elwick Road to the Registry Office. The ceremony was quite informal and nice, once completed we drove to Little Silver Hotel in St. Michaels for a private reception.

Life began to get unsettled and a bit difficult over the next few years. Bob was not very well. Although he made light of

*Julie and Robert's wedding 1994.*

it, with his usual mischievous quips and wit, he was suffering with his leg. His ankle never fully recovered. The hip was painful. An ulcer had caused more problems and he had spells of gout. This, on top of the high blood pressure which had dogged him for most of his adult life. He was on medication for the blood pressure and ulcer, plus painkillers which he washed down with a can of Gold Label (Barley-wine), nicknamed 'Hand Grenades' and other unprintable names. This mixture did not improve his temper and he could blow up at any time. Hence the 'hand grenades' saying. Nevertheless, he still helped out around the farm as best he could and still took day trips to France with his mates.

He became very ill. I had to force him to see the doctor by making the appointment myself. He adamantly said he would not go. I told him, in that case, he himself must cancel the appointment. He saw the doctor who diagnosed a lung infection and water retention. Bob said he had not drunk any water. Leaving the surgery he went straight to his 'office', the Vine pub for a pint of beer, where he stated he was the quality surveyor.

Life with Bob had always been a roller coaster. Never a dull moment, with plenty of fun and laughs but there were dark times too. By the mid-nineties, we had relinquished the meat poultry side of the business, due to Bob's disability and my bad back, which I had injured as a teenager. I slipped on a wet brick floor whilst carrying 1 cwt. (55 kilos) of grain on my back. I was regularly visiting an Osteopath, sometimes I could barely walk.

We still had laying hens, selling the eggs locally and of course, some geese for which I have always had a great liking. Their large white eggs always sell well during their short laying season from late January to the end of June, beginning of July. They will happily graze in awkward places unreachable with a mower, under fruit trees and tight corners. The only downside is their webbed feet which quickly flatten spring flowers - Daffodils and Tulips. Some sticks tied together will protect these.

At the beginning of August 1998, some more point-of-lay pullets were required. A friend at Faversham had some Black Rocks for sale. These birds, mainly black with gold-bronze feather around the throat area, were good layers and laid for a longer period of time than some hybrids. My daughter Julie needed some too. On Sunday, August 9th Robert, Julie's husband, drove us to collect the pullets. It was a hot day. The birds were put into their new homes and given ample water and left to settle and cool down.

The following day, August 10th was the hottest day of the year, temperatures reaching nearly 90°F. Groceries were needed and Bob wanted his usual pint, or two. So I drove us to Tenterden, returning home about noon in the scorching heat. Toby, the pony needed to come in from his paddock and the poultry needed water. This done, I returned to the bungalow to get lunch. Bob ordered some of the fresh baked bread and cheese and some of our home-grown tomatoes. Having consumed his lunch, he was attempting to read the Daily Mail with his chin cupped in his hands, elbows on the table. As he nodded off to sleep his elbows slipped from their position, thus waking him up. It was hot indoors, so I decided to find some shade in the garden. As I walked out the heat haze was visible across the paddock from where Toby had been. Finding shade beneath the oak and cherry trees, I sat down to rest on the grass. I dozed too, but was aroused by the dogs barking. Thinking there was a fox after the new pullets, I quickly got up to investigate. I needed my shoes. Hurrying indoors, I found Bob slumped in his chair at the table as I had left him. He had died – a heart attack, one week before his birthday.

Bob's funeral service was held on his birthday August 17th. St Mildred's Church Tenterden was packed full of mourners from all walks of life.

About ten days later, Julie, Robert and I, together with my close neighbours Gordon and Gill Lilly, scattered Bob's ashes in his favourite place, alongside the lake, deep in the valley. In his natural habitat so to speak. Here he could keep an eye on all the surrounding wildlife, the fish in the clear water, the silver-grey heron gliding on outstretched wings, dropping slowly onto the bank, wading into the water on long legs. A flash of blue, a kingfisher also hunting fish. On the water too, is a late hatch of Mallard duck, propelling themselves like little speedboats, catching midges and flies. Suddenly a cock pheasant shouts "cock-up" as he flutters and reaches a branch, signalling a red fox stealthily negotiating the under-growth, while rabbits run, their white tails bobbing as they safely reach the burrow. At night, the badger comes snuffling along searching for worms and grubs. There are blackberries in abundance, pushing down the brambles with bear-like feet, they eat greedily. The tawny owl hoots. A sheep baa's in the distance, answered by the moo from a cow. Rest in Peace. We had been married for 36 years.

I decided to give myself four or five years before making any decision about my future.

*The Lake at Mill Pond Farm after escavation was complete.*

*The Lake after it had become established. Bob's ashes were scattered there.*

# Holidays

We did not have family holidays at all when we were children. Livestock cannot be left unattended, but we did have family days out in the summer to the seaside. Camber or Jury's Gap were preferred to Hastings, due to their sandy shores as opposed to the pebbles/stones at Hastings.

My most memorable and lovely trips were on summer evenings when Joan and I would walk with Mum and Dad with David and Christine in a pushchair to one of the Tenterden pubs, usually the Black Horse (now the William Caxton). Sometimes as far as the Fat Ox in St Michaels. We would all be given a bag of Smiths crisps with salt contained in a piece of blue paper screwed tight to close it, and a glass of lemonade while parents had a glass of beer. The best part was walking back home along the lane in the moonlight with the nightingales singing, the glow-worms shining on the grass verge and the smell of the honeysuckle in the hedge. This vivid memory will stay with me forever.

At Christmas time a taxi would be hired for a trip to Maidstone for Christmas shopping. Lunch was eaten at the County Hotel and later it was off to visit Father Christmas in his grotto in one of the larger stores. Grandfather stayed home just to keep an eye on things.

Grandfather was a member of Tenterden Working Men's Club and him being a member, Joan and I were able to join a coachload of youngsters to visit a pantomime.

Another London trip 1954-55 was when my aunt who bred racing greyhounds had some to sell and we travelled up in a cattle lorry with the dogs to an auction. After the sale, we went to the London Palladium to see Norman Wisdom. The only seats available were 'up in the Gods' – really high up at the back. I remember my mother was terrified hanging on to her seat for dear life fearing she was going to fall.

My first proper 'holiday' was in the summer of 1959 when I was 20. My sister Joan was working at Little Fowlers Nursing Home in Hawkhurst in the catering department. Joan became friendly with another employee, Maureen, who lived in Hawkhurst. Maureen had a cousin living on the Isle of Wight. Maureen was due to have a holiday, planning to visit her cousin who was heavily pregnant. My sister was invited to go with Maureen for two weeks. Plans were set in motion but when the Matron of the home found out, she refused to let Joan go because it would create a staff shortage. I was invited to take Joan's place which I readily accepted. Now it was my turn to make plans.

This would be an adventure for me. I had never been away from home before. The day arrived, bright sunny and warm. Summer dresses and swimming costumes had been packed. Maureen came to Tenterden where we caught the bus to Hastings, then the train into the unknown, towns and countryside whizzing past at great speed until we reached Portsmouth. There the ferry was waiting for the final leg of the journey to Ryde. Welcoming us were beautiful gardens with flowers spelling out the word 'RYDE'.

Maureen's cousin lived in Cowes, the home of the biggest yachting regatta. Ships of every size, colours and creed filled the marina. So far, so good. When we eventually arrived at the cousin's property, it turned out to be a pokey, cramped second-floor flat with small rooms and windows that let in little light.

The cousin had been taken to the hospital because the birth was imminent and she had some complications. After settling in I rang home to let everyone know we had arrived safely.

The next evening Maureen went to visit her cousin while I took a walk around the neighbourhood and through a park-like recreation ground. There I was accosted by some local yob-type bloke who tried to chat me up! I had to let him know, in no uncertain terms that I was definitely not interested.

A few days later the baby arrived safely. Maureen and I were then able to explore the island. We purchased train tickets which enabled us to travel all around the island – completed in one day. Over the course of the next week we visited Alum Bay, renowned for its multi-coloured sands; Blackgang Chine with gnome garden; sunbathed and swam at Sandown and marvelled at the shining white rocks of the Needles protruding from the sea. In no time at all, it was time for the return journey home and back to normality and work.

I have mentioned that Bob and I spent our honeymoon in Looe, Cornwall. We really enjoyed the West Country, it being so rural, we were often held up by a flock of sheep on the narrow lanes.

In the summer of 1972, after haymaking was complete, Bob and I managed to get a week off. We took Ann and Julie to Cornwall and showed them the sights that Bob and I had seen ten years earlier. The girls enjoyed playing in the silvery sands and walking on the Banjo Pier.

On our return journey, we drove across Dartmoor with all the beauty this National Park has to offer. The flat moor with rough grasses and heather, a dark tor in the distance, but most interesting to the girls were the wild ponies. Really they were not that wild, now being accustomed to vehicles and tourists as the photos show.

My last holiday, so to speak, was in 2005. My nephew Vernon Pilcher, Christine's younger son was living and working in the 'Emerald Isle'. There he had met this beautiful blond girl of his dreams, Emer Dunne. They decided to make

*< On the Isle of Wight holiday in 1959, aged 20.*

*Bob, Julie and Ann in Dartmoor 1971.*

*Some very friendly Dartmoor ponies.*

*This foal was trying to chew a 'cat's eye'.*

*Julie and I at Barberstown Castle, Ireland in 2005.*

*< The Irish National Stud entrance.*

*> Julie visiting the stallion boxes.*

a go of life and get married. Vernon was living in Clondalkin, near Dublin. The wedding was to be held in the Roman Catholic church there.

The date was set for Monday, June 6th, a bank holiday in Ireland. Julie and I were invited. It was decided that we would fly out on the Saturday, June 4th. A great deal of work and preparation was required before departure. Firstly, I needed someone to look after Mill Pond Farm in my absence. Livestock-wise there were 100+ hens, 12 ducks, 15 geese, 4 dogs, pony Toby and Julie and Robert's cattle. Robert very kindly agreed to look after everything with the aid of Gill and Gordon Lilly, my neighbours, who had the task of letting the dogs out thrice daily - Mixer (Jack Russell, 17yrs), her offspring fathered by the Collie, Dot and Otto (13 years) and Dot's daughter Minty (8 years).

Although Mixer was ageing, they were still quite a formidable quartet. They had a large fenced enclosure in which to run. With the bungalow front door open and a large Leylandii outside, they had the best of both worlds.

Robert would feed them when he came late afternoon. I had cooked and frozen meals for them.

Shopping trips to Ashford and Headcorn in search of dresses and other accessories were eventually successfully completed. I needed a passport because at the time it was unclear if one could enter Ireland without. The only previous passport I had had was one of those little green paper things which allowed travel into France and Belgium etc.

Flights were booked with Ryanair and Euros bought at Tenterden Post Office.

The wedding reception was to be held at Barberstown Castle, County Kildare. Julie and I booked in there for convenience.

This trip meant several 'Firsts' for me, including:

1. First enduring passport.
2. First time flying, and only time.
3. First time visiting Ireland.

With everything in place and bags packed to the limit, Saturday, June 4th dawned bright and sunny but with the risk of a shower, I went about my usual morning routine of feeding and watering all the poultry. I turned Toby out into his little paddock. His grazing had to be restricted or he would succumb to laminitis. I mucked out his stable and filled a hay net. The dogs were always with me while doing these tasks. While I checked the cattle they would hunt rabbits in the hedges and wood. A sharp whistle usually brought them bounding back. Breakfast time for me now. The time passed quickly. Soon I was saying goodbye to the dogs, they had never been left on their own before. Hopping into my old blue Citroen Saxo, I was driving, on my way through Rolvenden to Sandhurst to Julie and Robert's farm. The car would remain there until we returned. Robert drove us to Gatwick to catch the plane. I was a little anxious about flying. I am not a good traveller, being prone to travel sickness. The flight did not affect me. The aerial view soon after take-off was magnificent. The countryside looked beautiful, with patchwork fields of green, yellow and brown. The tree canopies stood out as did some of the buildings. Soon, as we gained altitude, land disappeared and we were riding the clouds – big white fluffy ones and others smaller, tinged with grey. Then over the Irish sea, descending into Dublin airport. After collecting our luggage Julie and I found Christine and Ivan as arranged and we were on the road again heading for Barberstown Castle.

After checking into our room, freshening up and a change of clothes the time had come for our evening meal. Following earlier directions, down the wide staircase along a corridor to where a sign read 'Bar and Dining Room'.

A barman greeted us and provided a drink, showed us to an adjoining room, square in shape, cosy with dark furniture. A waiter presented us with menus and returned a little while later to take our order. We had chosen a window table which overlooked a garden. Perfectly mown green lawns with rose beds and a tree backdrop. Taking in our new surroundings and sipping our drinks, the waiter returned quite quickly, placing a plate before each of us. "With the Chef's compliments," he remarked. What culinary delicacy had we here? Oysters! Julie and I looked at each other. Ugh! Neither of us could stomach these slimy, nauseous molluscs. There was nowhere to dispose of these offensive objects. The waiter returned. A look of horror when he saw the uneaten shellfish. Trying to apologise, my words came out all wrong when I mumbled, "Sorry, all due respects to the chef, but we cannot eat them". His face went from horror to glower. Realising I had probably insulted the chef, I swiftly added, "We can't eat them because they upset our stomachs". The waiter snatched the plates from the table and disappeared in a huff. He returned with our main course, but a young waitress served our dessert.

Later, walking the long corridor, Julie and I stopped to admire some paintings when our young waitress joined us. I explained to her about the oysters, hoping that nobody had been offended. She laughed and said, "Not to worry. I will see that you are not given oysters tomorrow evening". Wishing each other 'goodnight', we went our separate ways.

The next day, Sunday was fine and a little warmer. After breakfast, no hiccups here, we joined Christine and Ivan to visit the Irish National Stud and the Japanese Gardens. Christine wanted to tour the gardens, Julie and I couldn't wait to visit the stud. Agreeing to meet up for lunch, we embarked on our sightseeing. The stud stables were palatial, immaculate, nothing out of place, not even a piece of straw in the yards.

This is the home of some of the most famous racing thoroughbreds in the world. Two of the stallion boxes were occupied by *Verglas* and *Invincible Spirit.*

Two foaling boxes housed two new-born foals.

Owners send their pregnant mares here for the foal to be delivered and then covered (mated) as soon as she comes into season.

Outside in the post and rail fenced, lush green paddocks can be seen retired stallions *Vintage Crop* and *Danioli.* Mares with young foals, cavorting and grazing. A fantastic sight.

The Irish Horse Museum was opened in 1977. Its centre-piece is the skeleton of *Arkle*, the great steeplechaser, who won 23 races including three successive wins in the Cheltenham Gold Cup, beating the mighty *Mill House.* The stud was also home to *Tulyar*, Derby winner 1952 and *Nijinsky* the last triple crown winner (2000 guineas Derby and St Leger) ridden by Lester Piggott, and *Northern Dancer*, winner of the Kentucky Derby U.S.A. in 1964. Also memorabilia of some of the greatest jockeys, including Sir Gordon Richards.

In the evening the rest of the family arrived for a meal. The venue was inside the castle roundel. The stone walls were decorated with hunting trophies, stags heads, rifles and knives.

Starters were served. No, Julie and I didn't receive oysters, instead, it was Paté de Fois Gras - goose liver pate! This was not very appetising either, but with plenty of fresh bread and a glass of wine and lots of laughter, we ate it.

Wedding Day - Monday, June 6th. A lovely day for a bank holiday wedding. As I had not witnessed a Roman Catholic ceremony, I expected it to be quite strict and formal.

It was, in fact, a lovely relaxed ceremony which the whole congregation enjoyed.

The reception at Barberstown Castle began with a meal. An Irish band and dancers entertained all until about midnight. The next day, Tuesday, all of the family flew back to Gatwick. Robert was there to meet us. Hugging us both together he exclaimed, "You're never going to do that again". Out on the road, heading home, Robert said to me. What do you want first, the bad news or the good news?" "Better tell me the bad news" I replied. "Nothing too bad" he responded. "Just that the dogs had dug out of their run and were looking for you" and "Don't those ducks make a bloody mess?".

# A New Beginning

It was at the beginning of 1999, I had a glut of hens eggs. Needing another outlet, I joined the newly-formed Rolvenden Farmers Market. It was unique as it was held in Rolvenden Church. Boards were laid across the pews to form tables from which vendors sold their produce. From eggs to meat, fruit, veg, cakes, wool and some craft items with light refreshments available. Customers walked the aisle to browse, peruse and buy from this colourful array of stock. This was my Thursday morning occupation for about seven years. At its height I was selling eggs from 150 hens. Farmers Markets sprang up in nearly every local village reducing the number of customers, meaning for me it was unviable. I found another outlet in Ward & Son Butchers at Benenden.

In 2014 the opportunity arose for me to sell Mill Pond Farm. February 2015 saw the sale agreed with completion in October. The time had come to clear out nearly 43 years of junk and look for another home. Ideally, I wanted a bungalow with 4-5 acres to keep some chicken and the geese and for the dogs to run free.

The fruitless search ended when I learned that Little Halden Place Farm was for sale. The property of Mary and Michael Orpin. Their estate agent, Richard Thomas, asked if I knew it. Of course, I did, being the same age as Michael Orpin, Heronden is only about two miles away cross country. Plus, I spent the first five years of my married life on the ad-joining farm, Goodshill House Farm. The distance to the North East, from Goodshill to Mill Pond Farm, as the crow flies, is barely a mile. I had not been on Little Halden Place for about thirty years. My first viewing of the property was on July 14th on what would have been our 53rd wedding anniversary. As I stepped out of the car that lovely sunny afternoon, I looked towards Potts Farm, the fields bathed in golden sunlight, the big, round freshly baled hay seemed to wink at me, inviting me.

Julie joined me and we were given a quick look at the bungalow which was surrounded by a garden, mostly lawn and somewhat overgrown. The buildings although useful, were mainly, in my opinion, unsightly. The yard area was a collection of old broken down vehicles, shipping containers and caravans. The property also had a Caravan Club C.L. site. The property had not been actively farmed for more than 30 years due to the owner's ill health. The fields were unkempt with White Robin grass gone to seed. Fences were practically non-existent. The buildings were crammed with clutter. The one saving grace is its breathtaking views from beyond the buildings. Looking East is Potts Farm, then Tenterden church, glorious in the afternoon sun, it appears so close that it is touchable. In panoramic fashion, open countryside is visible right around to Rolvenden including its church, St Mary the Virgin.

*The incredible views from Little Halden Place Farm land.*

Now I am in a quandary. Really it is too big, 30 acres and some of the buildings need repair. Two days later I returned with Robert (son-in-law). We decided that I would make an offer. The offer was rejected. I then enlisted the professional help of my estate agent, Alan Mummery. After much deliberation, weighing up the pros and cons, Alan and I thought the land would be my best investment. After five previous nights with little sleep, despite the fact that the property did not tick all the boxes, I decided to go for it and the sale was agreed. The main attributes being I would still abide in my hometown of Tenterden, plus after living all my life on the land, I still needed the grass under my feet.

Now I faced the biggest challenge of my life to restore Little Halden Place Farm to its former glory of a good working farm. I reckoned it would take at least three years. Telling my accountant about the deal he said, "Yes, but how many men in white coats do you have waiting at your gate?"

The completion date was October 14th, 2015. When I walked into the empty bungalow that afternoon, I was utterly dismayed to find it needed a great deal of redecorating and I wished I had never seen the place. With the aid of Julie and Robert and his mate David, a plumber, a decorator and a carpet fitter, the bungalow was partially habitable by November 21st. It was moving day. It dawned wet and miserable, just as it was when Bob and I moved into Mill Pond Farm. This time it snowed as well. At least we had Robert's cattle trailer in which to move, as opposed to the open tractor-trailer when occupying Mill Pond. I had been on my own at Mill Pond for 17 years, much more than I anticipated and had lived there for 43 years.

I found the move extremely unsettling. It was not home. I hated the noisy traffic and was fearful of the dogs getting on the road. Gradually, I got used to and overcame the strangeness of it all. The caravan site has brought a lot of new people from all over this country, and abroad too. I have found some special friends also – David and Michelle Ward and son Nick and Peter and Roni Orpin. Peter kindly drew the illustrations for this book. Over the last two years I have worked harder than ever and with Julie and Robert and others too numerous to mention, we have achieved much towards our goal. My reward is the praise and compliments received.

This will be my last home.

*Other titles available by Evelyn Luck:*

*As Luck Would Have it   -     ISBN: 9787770064241.*

*With Silas, Sam and Dodger at Little Halden Place Farm.*

## Acknowledgements

Evelyn Luck gratefully acknowledges being able to use the following images in this publication:

| | | |
|---|---|---|
| Geoff Partner | - | Standard Fordson with spade lugs |
| Charlie Light (Chick) | - | Charcoal Burning |
| Peter & Roni Orpin | - | Church View photo |
| Bingham Appliances (B.I.) Ltd | - | Bingham Plucking Machine |
| Peter Orpin | - | Tool Illustrations |
| Neil Ridley | - | Harvesting photos |
| "     " | - | Thatched House, Smarden |
| "     " | - | Last Hop Measure |
| "     " | - | Threshing Machine |
| Paul Harvey | - | Stacking Bundles of Thatching Straw |
| Richard Filmer | - | Cutting Corn with Binder |
| Alamy Stockphotos | - | Suffolk Punch Horses |
| Tenterden & District Museum | - | Hop Picking in Tenterden |
| "     " | - | Mr G Crouch with Hop Pockets |
| Jack Gillett | - | Pictures of Allen's shop |
| Trevor Mitchell | - | Dig for Victory |
| K.E.S.R | - | Tenterden Railway picture. |

And extends her thanks to Anna Foster for starting her off with this book, Colin Roberts who has now sadly passed, Gordon Lilly, Shirley and Jim Reeves and anyone else she may have omitted who helped or inspired her.

*Myself with Julie and the seat which I presented to Tenterden in Bob's memory on June 2nd 1999 with inscription.*

*Ill gotten gains! Receiving 1st prize for chickens Julie had entered in the Ashford Fatstock Show in 2000.*

Printed in November 2021
by Rotomail Italia S.p.A., Vignate (MI) - Italy